Indian Fiction In English Translation

INDIAN FICTION IN ENGLISH TRANSLATION

Edited by
SHUBHA TIWARI

ATLANTIC
PUBLISHERS & DISTRIBUTORS (P) LTD

Published by
ATLANTIC
PUBLISHERS & DISTRIBUTORS (P) LTD
7/22, Ansari Road, Darya Ganj, New Delhi-110002
Phones : +91-11-40775252, 40775214, 23273880, 23275880
Fax: +91-11-23285873
Web: www.atlanticbooks.com
E-mail: orders@atlanticbooks.com

Printed & bound in India by Atlantic Print Services

Preface

The study of Indian culture, ethos, Indian ways of life and thinking, her history and heritage shocks a researcher. In recent times, there have been efforts to present Indian culture in a presentable package. The aimed consumer of these exercises has been the Western World. But India is not such an easy phenomenon. When we study Indian literature in English translation, we are surprised to discover our own land, her beauty as well as her weaknesses. We realize that India is neither a *tyag, tapasya* type of land nor is it totally indoctrinate and materialistic. There are so many layers of existence of this ancient yet modern and ever changing land. The experiences of the people of this country find candid expression in Indian literature. It becomes a fascinating study.

In the first piece of this anthology, Prof. A.D.N. Bajpai tries to see the study of literature and role of translation from a different perspective. Basically a lecture, the piece voices certain original ideas regarding reality, its reflection in literature, and its transportation by translation. Prof. R.N. Rai underlines the importance of translation in his paper. Instead of highlighting its problems, he touches upon the common qualities of all languages and their inherent nature to be easily and beautifully translated into another language. Prof. B.N. Singh, discusses the autobiographies of Amrita Pritam as they appear in their translations. His stress is on the confessional mode of Pritam's style. The next paper is again on Amrita Pritam. Prof. Jagdev Singh probes the phenomenon of partition and its impact on the most innocent non-partisan, especially women. The theme of partition dominates the next paper also where Prof. M.P. Sinha discusses Qurratulain Hyder's *Fireflies in the Mist*. The paper brings to light the trauma of partition experienced across the border in Pakistan. The next paper by Prof. B.G. Tandon is a poetic representation of the element of *karuna* (compassion) in the short stories of Tagore. I have tried to analyze one short story by Intizar Husain. I have tried to capture the postmodernist approach of the writer. Sadhana Agrawal has dealt with man-woman relationship in the Hindi classic *Godan* by Prem Chand. "Woman in *Deodas"* by Dr. Ranjana Chanana describes the bold place occupied by women in *Deodas,* in particular, and in all novels of Saratchandra in general. The next two papers are by Dr. Vijay Prakash Singh, of which one analyses *Pather Panchali* as the song of Bengal's common life while the another compares two story-tellers from South—Masti and Basheer. Dr. Neelanjan Pathak probes into the fundamental concepts of vice and virtue with reference to Pratibha Ray's short story *Transgression*. Dr. Shobha Diwakar has analyzed another short story *Beast* by Chitra Mudgal. Dr. Manjunatha Bevinakatti has gone into the folklore of Karnataka with reference to certain texts. Dr. Aliya Shobi has brought out the humanistic approach of the short-story-teller Manoj Das. Lastly, Kiran Shukla in her paper goes into the trauma of a mother whose son is lured into Naxalite movement depicted in *Hajar Chaurashir Ma* by Mahasweta Devi. Overall here is a bouquet that brings India for you. It is of interest to those who are proud of India and believe in the identity that is Indianhood.

SHUBHA TIWARI

CONTENTS

1

LITERATURE, FICTION AND TRANSLATION

A.D.N. BAJPAI

We all know the tremendous power and potential of literature. Literature is a source of transformation not only in the personality of its reader but also that of the whole society. One function that literature performs and that interests me is sublimation of instincts. It makes one a normal human being. Only with sufficient insight into literature, study of literature, be it Sanskrit, Hindi or English, deep knowledge of knack and nuances of literature, we can translate our instinctual behaviour into normal behaviour. In my view, the process of sublimation is not possible without reading literature. On the other hand, the written word cannot be called literature if it does not sublimate the instincts of its readers. For example, reading of Sanskrit literature brings about tremendous sublimation. Its sublimity brings sublimation in the minds and hearts of its readers. The element of sublimity and the effect of sublimation differentiates literature from instinctual writing.

In this connection, let us remember that there is a basic difference between Indian literature and India's literature. Whatever written in India may be called Indian but it cannot be called India's. A literary creation has to have our cultural ethos, some properties of Indian soil to be called India's literature. The biggest differentiating feature in India's culture is her spiritualism. Our thrust on soul and the role of spirit are the factors that make India, her culture and literature so unique and elevated.

The dictionary meaning of fiction is 'literary creation of imagination'. It denotes something other than reality. But no writing on earth can be away from reality. The roots of all artistic creations lie in reality. Reality, too, has many types—realized reality, reality of pre-births, reality experienced by our ancestors, and finally reality that is yet to come. Realized reality covers all the experiences of the writer as well as those around her/him. A creator has the potential to experience not only what is happening to her/himself but to others as well. A creator knows the joys and pains not only of her/himself but also those of others. A writer is a sensitive soul. She/he is capable of catching the very nerve of others' heart. I can talk about the second type of reality quite comfortably as a Hindu. I believe that the experiences and doings of previous births come in the form of genes in a new born baby. There is no tabula *rasa*. The slate of soul is always full of writings from our preceding births. There is no void—even the void is pregnant with thundering ideas. This connectivity of births is what makes 'death' a new beginning in the Hindu thought. The third type of reality is contained in all the reservoirs of traditional wisdom—our Vedas, Upanishads, Puranas, and other sacred texts. These writings affect the present-day writing in more ways than one. They constitute the collective psyche. We may not realize consciously but they do shape and form our literary creations. Finally, there is a reality that is to come. Writers are prophets; they can see the future. There are so many instances where the premonitions of writers have proved to be true. I think that the writings of the French seer, Nostradamus which are so popular these days can be seen in this light only. Similarly, whatever Tulsidas said about Kalyug in *Sri Ram Charit Manas* is proving to be true word by word. Prophecy is nothing but sharpening of intellect, reasoning and logic. One inference leads to another and in this manner we have a chain of predictions. Outer variables can change the outcome to some extent but, by and large, future can be experienced by a talented writer. It is all a matter of flowing in the stream of time—past, present, and future are the blocks of the same string. The acute experiencing of one can lead to experiencing of another. It is rather a simple technique.

Borrowing from one form of reality to create another is not new to us. There are certain Sanskrit shlokas that Tulsidas translated *ad verbatim* into Avadhi and yet he remained as original as the writer of those shlokas. For example:

मूकं करोति वाचालम्, पंगु लंघयते गिरिम्
यत्कृपा तमहं वन्दे, परमानन्द माधवम्।
These lines have been written like this,
मूक होय वाचाल, पंगु चढ़इ गिरिवर गहन
जासु कृपा सो दयाल, करहु कृपा मर्दन-मयन।
Another example is, 'यदा यदा हि धर्मस्य'
translated as, 'जब जब होई धरम कै हानी'।

It is simply how intensely you have felt the words of the writer, how sincerely you have digested the essence of a particular writing and then reproduced. The creation of a writer does not remain her/his own; it becomes the reader's property. The process of translation and the role of the translator are not far from this. A translator is as much a creator as the writer of the original text. If the translator has imbibed the spirit of a literary creation, its background and cultural ethos, the translation will be good. There are even examples where a translated piece is better than the original. We can only imagine the state of Gurudev Rabindranath Tagore when he translated his *Geetanjali* into English, for which, he received the Nobel Prize. It is the complete involvement of the translator in the process of translation that is important. When the translator undergoes 'trance' while translating, a good work is born. The entire synergy of the translator comes out while translating a piece she/he loves.

Once the great Sanskrit poet, Banabhatta, who lived in our Vindhya region only near Sidhi, faced severe hitch in completing his classic 'Kadambari'. He wanted someone, especially one of his sons to complete it. He called his eldest son and asked him to translate a simple sentence into Sanskrit. The sentence was—ये सूखा पेड़ सामने है।

The son translated it like this—शुष्कः वृक्षः तिष्ठति अग्रे।

The poet dismissed his eldest son. Then he called the younger one and asked him to translate the very same sentence. The younger one translated it like this—नीरत तरुवर विलसीत पुरूतः।

Banabhatta marked the younger son as the right person to write 'Kadambari'. In fact, translation is not merely word to word translation. The entire synergy of the individual personality is involved in this process. Emotions are to be grasped, the mode of expression is to be caught, the mood and momentum of the words are to be captured and whole civilization that speaks through a work is to be understood—this, by no standard, is an ordinary task.

At the practical level, a translator has to take many precautions. Personal likes and dislikes play a vital role in the formation of literary creations but while they can be given full vent in creating one's own text, they have to be kept aside in translation. Being true to the original text is the first and foremost prerequisite of translation. A translator cannot stress a point s/he likes and cannot ignore something s/he does not like. Choice of words is equally important. Vocabulary for serious discourse and for humorous writing is entirely different and is not interchangeable. Same is the case for romantic, tragic, historical, and other types of pieces. While translating Kalidas, you cannot say, 'A gal got bonkers seeing clouds and jumped with chums.' Appropriate choice of words is crucial indeed.

An important aspect of translation in within language translation. Avadhi, Hindi, Bhojpuri, Brij, Baghelkhandi, Bundelkhandi—all to be mutually translated create a complex phenomena. Keeping the richness of India's lingual traditions, translation within different dialects of Hindi becomes very relevant. We search the world without knowing our own intellectual wealth. Similarly, translation among Indian languages like Hindi, Telugu, Tamil, Oriya, Kannada and others must not pose much problem as they all originate from Sanskrit. We can easily find suitable words in these languages. But when it comes to translation between Hindi and English and other foreign languages, it becomes difficult to find parallel expressions because the origin of English and foreign languages is different. The cultural background is so important in translation of literary pieces. Translation between Hindi and Urdu becomes easy because of the sameness of cultural milieu. The ethos, cultural background and history unite the two languages and translation becomes flowing and smooth.

With the growing popularity of convent education, a very common phenomenon among young Indians is that the richness of our ancient knowledge often startles them. They know Nancy Drew series of detective stories and every detail of Harry Potter's stories but fail to grasp the utter practicability of Kautilya's *Arthshastra* or attraction of *Kathasaritsagar*. Translation is one medium that can connect these rootless generations to our soil and also bring about national integration. The depth and magnanimity of Tamil, Marathi, Konkani, Oriya, Bangla and all other Indian literatures can be brought into main stream by effective use of translation.

I am convinced that the more we know our motherland, the more we will love her. The same logic extends to the whole world. Translation is a potent tool for transferring ideas, cultural values, traditional knowledge of ancient lands, as also the specific needs and aspirations of different peoples. Translation demolishes pre-conceived centres, brings the marginalized into focus and creates a just intellectual environment.

(The above piece contains excerpts from Prof. Bajpai's address at the seminar.)

2

Indian Fiction in English Translation: Problems and Perspectives

R.N. RAI

The proposed topic of UGC National Seminar—*Indian Fiction in English Translation* is not only interesting but challenging also. In the post-Independence era it is the need of the hour to project the genuine and authentic image of India to the outside world and it is possible only through English translation. Had Tagore's *Gitanjali* not been translated into English and with an Introduction by W.B. Yeats not submitted to Nobel Prize awarding Committee, it would perhaps not have been possible for Tagore to get the Nobel Prize in 1913. The world knows India through Indian writings in English but what about the genuine socio-cultural ethos that is presented through the writings in different Indian languages such as Hindi, Tamil, Telugu, Kannada, Oriya, Assamese, Bengali, Punjabi, Marathi and so many other regional languages of our country? How will people of the world come to know about the contribution of our Prem Chand, Nirala, Mahadevi, Jai Shankar Prasad, Fanishwer Nath Renu and so many others in Hindi, Padumaipittam, Madhaviah and Indira Parthasarthy in Tamil, Gopinath Mohanty in Oriya, Sarat Chandra, Tara Shankar Bandopadhayaya and Ashapurna Devi in Bengali, Amrita Pritam in Punjabi and so many other distinguished scholars who have written in other Indian languages? The only answer is that their works can be made available to the international readers through translation in English. Some admirable efforts have been made in this direction by Katha, Srishti, Rupa and Oxford University Press. New collections of English translation are brought out every year by them.

There is an urgent need to hold this kind of National Seminar on English translation of Indian Fiction, as the accuracy and authenticity of a translated text can be ascertained only by a person who is bilingual. The common reader who is even bi-lingual, hardly bothers to read the translated text in English. If one is well versed in Hindi (Hindi being his mother tongue), he will hardly bother to read Prem Chand's *Godan* or *Baban* in English translation. Now the question is: who will verify the authenticity of the translated text? It is possible only by a gathering of distinguished scholars who are bi-lingual and competent enough to assess the accuracy of the translated text. In this connection David Lodge in his book *Language of Fiction* (1966) has rightly remarked: "To test the closeness of any translation to its original, one would have to be not only bi-lingual but—to coin an ugly phrase—bicultural, i.e. possessed of the whole complex of emotions, associations and ideas which intricately relate a nation's language to its life and tradition, but possessed not only one such complex—as we are to some extent—but of two" (2).

Since English has increasingly become a global language, it has occupied the status of a significant 'communicative activity'. Referring to the growing importance of translation, Octavio Paz in "Translation of Literature and Letters," published in *Theories of Translation from Dryden to Derrida* (1992), has rightly pointed out that translation is "the principal means we have of understanding the world we live in" (154). Since most literary movements originate from and gain substance through repeated acts of translation, it is proper to understand the relevance and utility of translation. Translation transports the masterpieces of the human spirit from one language into another. It enriches the national language as well as literature. It renders the most important service to any literature as it makes the native speakers aware of the various forms of art and humanity and it widens the capacity for meaning and expression of one's own language. It is a great source of linguistic as well as cultural expansion. Looking back on the earlier history of translation in England, Graham Hough in his book *The Last Romantics* (1961) has rightly stated: "From the emergence of vernaculars to the break-up of European civilizations in our own day, translation was one of the most important means of maintaining a common culture" (71). In her book *Siting Translation* (1992) Tejaswini Niranjana has pointed out that in the opinion of Western literary critics at least since the Renaissance translation has been performing "the noble task of bridging the gap between peoples as the quintessential humanistic enterprise" (47).

If translation plays such an important role in the growth of human culture and civilization, what do we mean by translation? The literal meaning of the word translation is 'to carry across' from one language into another. In his book *A Linguistic Theory of Translation* (1965: 1, 20, 35-42) J.C. Catford defines translation as 'a process of substituting a text in one language for a text in another' involving the replacement of source-language meanings with alternative receptor-language meanings. Though each language has its own peculiarities, all languages have certain qualities in common which make 'translation' or 'transfer' of meaning from one language into another possible.

G. Devy in his article "Translation and literary history: An Indian View", published in *Post-colonial Translation* (1999) has aptly quoted J. Hillis Miller as saying "Translation is the wandering existence of a text in a perpetual exile" (182). The comment certainly refers to the Christian myth of the Fall, exile and wandering. In Western metaphysics translation is an exile, a fall from the origin, as it always comes into being *after* the original. The authorized translation of the Bible was regarded as a revolutionary event in the history of England, as the Protestant England sought the recovery of the original spirit of Christianity through translation of Bible.

In the late eighteenth century translation became part of the colonial discourse of Orientalism. In 1783 William Jones took his place on the bench of the Supreme Court in Calcutta and announced his motive of translating the Sanskrit texts. His motive was, as has been stated by Edward Said in his book *Orientalism* (1978) "to domestic the Orient and thereby turn it into a province of European learning" (78). His translations were widely read in the 19th century West, especially by the Germans—Goethe, Herder and others. Jones' translations of Kalidasa's *Sakuntala* and Manu's *Dharmasastra* were motivated by the following three reasons:

(i) Since Indians were not the reliable interpreters of their own laws and culture, translation was an immediate requirement for the Europeans.

(ii) Europeans wanted to 'purify' Indian culture and speak on its behalf.

(iii) Europeans wanted to be law-givers to Indians.

It is now a recognized fact that translation was an integral part of the European colonization, as colonization and translation moved hand in hand. Translation is not an isolated, innocent, transparent activity that operates in a vacuum, but, as S. Bassnett and Harish Trivedi in their Introduction to *Post-colonial Translation* have pointed out, "part of an ongoing process of intercultural transfer. Moreover, translation is a highly manipulative activity that involves all kinds of stages in that process of transfer across linguistic and cultural boundaries" (2).

The scenario in the Post-colonial era has changed. Since the Empire has now begun to write back to the centre, radical changes in the concepts of translation are taking place in the former colonies like India, Latin America, Canada and Ireland. They emphatically challenge the established European norms of translation. The superior European languages are freely interacting with the so-called marginalized languages of the developing countries. It is now an accepted fact that, as G. Devy has stated "the very foundation of modern Indian literature was laid through acts of translation, whether by Jayadeva, Hemchandra, Michael Mudhusudan Dutta, H.N. Apte or Bankim Chandra Chatterjee" (187).

The act of translation is no longer regarded as the Fall from Heaven, as inferior to the original. Translation, on the other hand, produces a new original in another language. The true test of translator lies in his capacity, says G. Devy, "to transform, to translate, to restate, to revitalize the original" (187). Translating a great work of art with precision and accuracy is just like 'walking on a razor's edge'. No text in its entirety can be fully translated. Any model translation has to fulfil the following basic requirements: adequacy, lucidity, consistency and completeness. Salman Rushdie does not agree with the commonly held view that 'something gets lost in translation'. He rather affirms that 'something can also be gained'. Translation is now viewed as an original creation in another language. It is used in the context of 'transcreation', 'Transluciferation', 'transtextualization', even 'poetic reorchestration'.

While translating the text, the translator has to face the following problems:

(i) He is supposed to be not only bi-lingual but if possible, bi-cultural also. He should be acquainted with the cultural norms of the society the source text is dealing with.

(ii) He is faced with the problem of translating the text from one verbal order to another verbal order within the same language system or from one language system to another language system or from one verbal order to another system of signs.

(iii) He is confronted with the problems coming in the way of translation when he has to translate between languages having differences at the grammatical, stylistic, lexical and socio-cultural level.

(iv) He has to handle features of the source culture such as objects, customs, mythical, historical and literary allusions which are not familiar to the receiving audience. Salman Rushdie has implicitly mentioned the myth of Shiva in *Midnight's Children* and it is quite possible that the significance of the myth of Shiva may be missed by non-Indian readers if it is not adequately explained.

(v) He has to solve the problem of equivalence if there are no equivalents available in the receptor culture. If he suppresses the distinctive qualities of the writer's culture and language and tries to adapt to the standards of the receiving culture, the question of 'fidelity' to the source text automatically arises.

(vi) The translator faces the problems with the proper names if they present unfamiliar phoneme or foreign sequences. He also faces the problems of transposing the literary genres, forms, proverbs and metaphors of the source culture.

(vii) Translation is said to be a kind of disguised commentary. It involves the process of judgment where 'objectivity' is almost impossible. Maria Tymoczko in her article "Post-colonial writing and literary translation," published in *Post-colonial Translation* has drawn our attention to this fact and rightly stated that "just as there can be no final translation, there can be no final interpretation of a culture through a literary mode" (24).

(viii) If the translator has to translate a dominant culture source text to a minority culture audience, he is free to leave dominant cultural materials implicit believing that the mythical, historical and cultural contexts might be known to the receptor audience. But when he has to translate a minority culture text for a dominant culture audience, he has to adopt certain devices to convey the full implications of the translated text.

Let us now see how these above mentioned problems of translation may be solved. They may be solved to a very great extent by adopting the following methods:

(i) In order to solve the problem of equivalents in the receptor language, the translator can use two words instead of one or a phrase or may resort to some other device in order to convey the full meaning of the source text. In this context Maria Tymoczko has suggested some solutions: "In the face of such a crux, a translator has a variety of choices: to omit the reference or pick some 'equivalent' in the receptor culture on the one hand, and on the other to import the word un-translated (with an explanation in a footnote perhaps), add an explanatory classifier or an explicit explanation, use a rare or recondite word of the receiving language, and so on" (25).

(ii) If mythical cultural contexts are to be made accessible to the receiving audience, it may be done either through explicit inclusion in the translation or through Para textual devices. It would, of course, ultimately result in the production of a longer text. The 'frontloading' cultural information or 'foregrounding' material would adversely affect the literary status of a text. The translated text would appear to be a didactive piece of work rather than a piece of imaginative literature.

(iii) Instead of following the letter of the original, the translator should catch its spirit and imagery and produce them freely in order to suit the new language. Sri Aurobindo is in favour of following the spirit of the text, as the literal translation often becomes flat and lifeless. Even Voltaire, while talking about literal translation, said: 'Letter killeth, but the spirit giveth life'.

(iv) In order to ensure the accuracy and reliability of the final version of translation, the translator should have a close reading of the original, a systematic study of its devices and effect, and follow a prolonged procedure of drafting, correcting and polishing the translated text. The most successful translation is the translation that is capable of making the most impressive rapport between widely separated people, places and times.

When we make a survey of Indian fiction, we do find that so many classics of Indian fiction such as Premchand's *Gaban* and *Godan,* Srilal Shukla's *Ragadarbari,* Jainendra's *Tyagapatra,* Nirmal Verma's *Wei Din,* Krishna Baldeo Vaidya's *Usaka Bachapan,* Ajneya's *Apne Apne Ajanawi,* U.R. Anantammuthy's *Sanskar,* Madhaviah's *Padmavati,* Indira Goswami's *The Shadow of Kamakhya,* Gopinath Mohanty's *Paraja,* Chandrasekhar Rath's *Yantrarudha,* Indira Parthasarthy's *Nandankhatai* have been translated into English, but it is a fact that many more are yet to be translated into English and other languages of the world. A comprehensive and systematic effort is needed to ensure that not only fiction but other genres of Indian literature are properly translated in order to make the world aware of the glorious aspects of our Indian literature. It is an undeniable fact that if Plato, Aristotle, Homer, Virgil, Dante, Pirandello, Tolstoy, Chekov, Brecht and other distinguished writers of the world had not been translated into English and other languages of the world, the world would have remained poorer than it is.

WORKS CITED

Catford, J.C. *A Linguistic Theory of Translation.* London: O.U.P., 1965.

Devy, G. "Translation and Literary History: An Indian View", *Post-colonial Translation* eds. S. Bassnett and Havish Trivedi. London: Routledge, 1999.

Hough, Grahm. *The Last Romantics.* London, 1961.

Lodge, David. *Language of Fiction.* London, 1966.

Niranjana, T. *Siting Translation.* Hyderabad: Orient Longman Ltd., 1995.

Paz, Octavio. "Translation of Literature and Letters", *Theories of Translation from Dryden to Derida* eds. R. Schulte and J. Biguenet. Chicago: University of Chicago Press, 1992.

Said, Edward. *Orientalism.* New York: Pantheon, 1978.

3

Confessional Outpouring of a Sensitive Soul: Reflections on Amrita Pritam's Autobiographies

B.N. SINGH

Amrita Pritam is a prolific writer and a versatile genius. Her essays, short stories and novels written in Hindi and Punjabi have been translated into more than thirty regional and foreign languages. Among the contemporary Indian writers she occupies a unique position. This 'uniqueness' arises because of her foray into both lovely and harsh visionary world which, apart from being confessional outpouring of a sensitive soul, is also a reflection on the patriarchal social constrains. The present paper is an attempt to understand the spoken/unspoken ordeal of Amrita Pritam as reflected in her two autobiographies *The Rasidi Ticket (The Revenue Stamp)*. The said autobiography captures her entire life in its fold. The confessional strains are very much evident herein that Amrita makes a candid confession of even the intimate experiences of her life she has undergone. Even a casual reading of autobiography suggests that all the experiences of her life since childhood have been created and lived under some shadow or another: the shadows of death, weapons, words, dreams, patriarchy, and shadows of authoritarian power, shadows of contemplation and shadows of unrequited love.

In a patriarchal social setup writing autobiography is indeed a very difficult task for a woman writer. Keeping in mind the social and cultural constraints Tharu and Lalita point out:

> Autobiography as a genre exhibits a certain ambivalence. The accent is on the personal. The existential contours

> of a life and the preoccupation with intimate, even confessional, detail often obscure the fact that autobiography always draws on the repertoire of life scripts that cultures provide at particular junctures in their history. Recurrent themes in many nineteenth-century memoirs are the woman's joy in the love and support of a progressive husband and her education and the new possibilities that opened out to her. But even in relatively conventional accounts we come across passages that give us a glimpse of many-faceted struggles involved: the pain of being constantly watched and corrected; the feeling that they were not good enough; the exhausting demands of the new housework; the uncertainty and anxiety involved in raising children in the new mode, outside the reassuring circle of the traditional family; the longing for the support of a world they had lost, and so on. (*Women Writing in India*, Vol. I, 160)

Amrita Pritam has woven a prodigious mass of personal experiences into the texture of her writings. It is necessary, therefore, to peep into those experiences of her life which have direct bearing on her writings. Her experience of growing up as a loner accounts for acute emotional vacuum in her writings. Her marital life was not successful, the evidences of which we very often get in her autobiographies and numerous other writings. Amrita Pritam's autobiographies, therefore, are a personal testimony of the new sense of worth she experienced as 'individual,' whose specific life is of interest and importance. Despite her preoccupation with intimate, even confessional aspects, she does not ignore the existential contours of life. The materials that she has gleaned from her personal experiences, whether real or visionary, have been converted into an artifact of beauty and order. Narrating the predicament of a woman writer Shobha De says:

> For a woman, a book in progress is like a secret lover she has to hide from her family and so people are terrified at the thought of writing about themselves. They find all kinds of excuses. They lie. They make up. They invent. They rub out. (*Selective Memory* 1-2)

"The worst aspect of writing", reminds Shobha De, "whether it's a memoir or a racy novel, is that you can't share the experience with anyone. It can be hellishly lonely sometimes. A feeling of such isolation, you ask yourself why you are punishing yourself like this. What for? There have to be better options" (*Selective Memory III*). Yet the expression of the self is a major feminist concern for her as "an unbearable pain reverberates through the entire body" (*Selective Memory III*). A woman autobiographer finds herself in this awful predicament due to the oppressive effects of patriarchy which maintains double moral standard toward sexes. This attitude gets manifested in women's autobiographies in both explicit as well as implicit ways. These spoken/unspoken ordeals, as pointed out by Shobha De, are very much pronounced in the autobiographies of Amrita Pritam.

The most conspicuous trait that is evident in Amrita's autobiographies is a woman's battle against authoritarian and male hegemonic discourse and her determination to "to dare to live the life she imagines". Her writing is celebrated for its sensuous imagery and evocative rhythm and is widely read and appreciated, though it has also been criticized as vacuous and sentimental. She writes:

> Society attacks anyone who dares to say its coins counterfeit, but when it is a woman who says this, society begins to foam at the mouth. It puts aside all its theories and arguments and picks up the weapon of filth to fling at her. (Quoted in Tharu and Lalita 160)

Her writings after 1960 deal more and more with women who acknowledge their desires and their independence and accept responsibilities for their lives even at the cost of love. Her mother was the sole inspiration behind this spirit of rebellion in her. Her mother, she writes, "never failed in the slightest degree to honour and obey my father's male will... [but] collected all the anger from her mind and poured it into my infant being. (Quoted in Tharu and Lalita 160)

Women writers have to resurrect and heal a self that has been mutilated by patriarchal constraints. In dealing with the chaos inflicted by society the woman writer glimpsed a power within her own psyche. In his preface to *Shadows of Words,* she writes:

> In the name of home, society, religion, and politics...those

> shadows were wrapped around the doors and walls. Somewhat deliberating, this book-reaches that desired destination—where the shadows of inner consciousness get translated into words. The symphony of this consciousness may not be captured in words—yet conserving about them are these few pages—which can be anointed as an inner journey. (Preface to *Shadows of Words*)

The said statement brings to the fore the nature and atmosphere of confessional strain in the *Shadows of Words*. One thing is obvious that words are adequate to give vent to her feelings: the shadows of inner consciousness have been translated into words. Further, the two dominant emotions which become explicit are that this autobiography is about 'inner consciousnesses' or 'inner journey' of the narrator. The inner journey ranges from "a demonic shadow which baptized me with thick smog" when she was "virtually standing alone in this strange world" (*Shadows* 1) to the spiritual enlightenment, "fervour of the fragrance within" (*Shadows* 140). In between is the experience of travail she has undergone because of her unrequited love for Sahir Ludhianvi, the noted Urdu poet. The teenager in Amrita Pritam is a sensitive soul, rather love-smitten and emotionally starved soul, the sufficient evidences of which we get in her autobiographies. The poems that she wrote in this age are the emotional outbursts of a love-lorn teenager who considered all the values which proved blocking stone on the pilgrim's highway of love as repressive. She has attached considerable importance to this phase when she experienced the first flush of youth. She wrote in *Rasidi Ticket*:

> In this, my sixteenth year, a question mark seemed to have erected itself against everything.... There were so many refusals, so many restrictions, so many denials in the air I breathed that a fire seemed to be smoldering in every breath I drew.... That sixteenth year is still present somewhere in every year of my life. (*Rasidi Ticket*)

As it has been mentioned earlier, also at sixteen, she married Gurbaksh Singh, editor of the Punjabi magazine *Preetlari*, to whom she had been engaged at the age of four with whom she had two children, Navraj and Kandia. Her husband's family was disturbed by the adverse publicity she often received, and wanted her to stop writing. And over a period of time, she has said in an interview with Madhu Kishwar and Ruth Vanita of the feminist journal *Manushi*, she realized that this marriage had not provided the companionship she had imagined and wanted. When her father died in 1940, she felt "absolutely alone".

The sixteenth year is the most precious and glorious but extremely turbulent phase of a youth's life. When the first flush of youth knocks at heart's door, turmoil begins within and without. Ironically, however, it creeps into mind and soul stealthily. Amrita describes the first touch of love in the sixteenth year of her age:

> Came my sixteenth year—like a stranger. Inside me, there was an awareness I could not explain....
>
> Like a thief, came my sixteenth year, stealthily like a prowler in the night, stealing in through the open window at the head of my bed.... (*The Revenue Stamp* 11)

The said passage is imbued with metaphorical implication. The description of the sixteenth year that follows is so emotional and poetic that it touches the heart. It characterizes the colossal emotional appetite of a teenager:

> Every *apsara* disturbing the meditations of a *rishi* was, myth logically speaking, the commissary of Lord Indras. My sixteenth year must also have been Lord Indra's work, invading the purity of my childhood. It was now that I began to write poetry, and on every poem I wrote, I carried the cross of forbidden desires. Just as the *rishis* became restless as each *apsara* appeared, so my rebellious thoughts pursued me, giving me no peace.... (*The Revenue Stamp* 12)

This beautiful dream and lovely imaginative vision emerge into ecstatic experience and she is transported into the world where bliss forever reigns. She thanks God for being trapped into the network of love, inflicting this pain, rather romantic pain, in her:

> I thank the fates that conspired to break through the years of my innocence. That conspiracy relates not only to that

> one year alone but to the whole of my life. (*The Revenue Stamp* 13)

However, despite having a "clandestine relationship" with this phase of life, this sixteenth year is also the year of awakening for Amrita when life took on a different meaning. It was the beginning of a new dawn, marked by a new awareness about life. A rebel in her challenged the orthodox, conservative and conformist attitude of society. Though nothing very significant happened, yet it marked a distinct phase in her life. She says:

> Yes life took on a different meaning, it was the beginning of an uneven road of life with all its hairpin bends, its ups and downs. It was also the beginning of curiosity. I questioned parental authority. I questioned the value of doing my work at school by rote. I questioned that had been preached to me and I questioned the entire stratified social scheme. What I had so far learnt was like a strait-jacket that gives way at the seams as the body grows. I was thirsty of life. I wanted living contact with those stars I had been taught to worship from afar. What got instead was advice and constraint which only fed my rebellion. (*The Revenue Stamp* 12)

The said passage is significant in that it outlines the future course that rebel in Amrita will take. 'Life took on a different meaning' suggests that she was going to be nonconformists questioning the 'entire stratified social scheme'. 'I was thirsty for life' suggests the acute emotional vacuum that had crept quite early in her life.

> Even now, everything around me seems to constrict the soul just as the clothes one grows out during adolescence. The lips are parched with the thirst for life; desire comes back to stretch the hand and touch the stars. Wherever in the world a wrong is done, I continue to feel a deep sense of outrage. (*The Revenue Stamp* 13)

She opines that everyone goes through this phase, but "it happened to me with three time's greater impact".

> First, there was the drabness of middle-class morality, then the dosage of "don'ts" thrust down my throat which I somehow felt I would have been spared, had my mother

> been alive. Here was the overbearing presence of my father, a man of religion. Poor Father. He wanted me to be an obedient, self-effacing daughter and here was I in my sixteenth year bearing my cross like the pang of an unfulfilled love. I was sixteen and the memory creeps into every phase of my life. (*The Revenue Stamp* 13)

Out of several precious moments which both enlighten and consume her heart is the memory of unrequited love for Sahir. Because of the conservative family milieu and its hatred toward Muslim there existed hatred between the two. Amrita recalls an incident whenever her father's Muslim friends visited her house, they were offered tea in glass tumblers which were kept away from all other pots and pans on a shelf in the corner of the kitchen, in their 'ostracized niche'. The rebel in Amrita could not tolerate this and she revolted against this custom of her father and grandmother: "thereafter, not a single utensil was labeled 'Hindu' or 'Muslim'" (*The Revenue Stamp* 5). She says:

> Deep down in the layers of my mind, was the first impact of a religion against which I had risen as a child, when I had seen that glass tumbler touched by someone with a different faith became impure. (*The Revenue Stamp* 150)

Ironically, however, she confesses: "Neither Grandmother nor I knew then that the man I was to fall in love with would be of the same faith as the branded utensils were meant for." (*The Revenue Stamp* 5)

The said confession brings her passionate longings for Sahir as "love, all alike nor season knows nor clime"; in other words, it transcends cultural and religious boundaries. Its worth becomes supreme even if it remains at platonic level, even if it is visionary, "Shadows are related to entities; they are subservient to entities" even if they do not fit into any such pattern. Her poignancy of feelings has been expressed in the following words:

> Young as I was, I wonder whether the shadow of my fate had not so been cast on me already.... Shadows have a reality longer than is recognized. Faces too have reality. But for how long? Shadows for as long as you like. For a lifetime, if you will.

> Years come and go. They do not wait. Some shadows, on the other hand, hover around is with an existence of their own.
>
> Sometimes it seems as a shadow is cast on you from nowhere. Broken away, it falls in your path, and you have to carry it along with you to whichever part of the world you go – in search of the entity from which it broke off. (*The Revenue Stamp* 5)

It is the 'shadow' of Amrita's first meeting with Sahir that haunts her and kept on haunting throughout her life. Her passionate longings for Sahir remained a constant source both her hopes and despair. She missed him much in life, but bore the pangs of bereavement with stoical fortitude. Her feelings find expression in one of the most beautiful and telling passages of *The Revenue Stamp*:

> Wayfarer! Why did you the first time meet me at an evening hour!
>
> I am approaching the turning point of my life.
>
> If you had to meet me at all why did you not meet me at high noon
>
> When you have felt its heat. (39)

The said lines are not written by Amrita but were recited by a famous Hindi poet Shiv Mangal Singh Suman. These lines touch the heart and so she comments about the universal feelings that these lines evoke, "each feels his own pain. But sometimes such pains bear striking similarities. These longings of mine have been bruised against that stern citadel of yours in the same city of my earlier hopes." (*The Revenue Stamp* 39)

In 1944 Amrita met the poet Sahir Ludhianvi. She describes the meeting in "Akhri Khat" (Last Letter), which, she says, was written as a story only because it could not be posted as a letter to Sahir. "My beloved," it ends, "this is the last letter I shall write to you...now with these hands kissed by you I will write songs not of silk but of iron.... When you read these battle songs remember I am writing them with the hands you have kissed." They enjoyed a long and mutually supportive friendship, but Amrita declared her love for him only in her poetry. The long poem "Sunehere" (Message), for which she won the Sahitya Akademi Award in 1953 and many other poems in her early collections were inspired by their friendship. She recalls an incident when a press photographer came to her with the news of Akademi Award for *Sunehere.* This testifies to the depth and intensity of her love for Sahir:

> Late that evening, came a reporter and a photographer from the press. The photographer wanted me to pose as one engrossed in the act of writing. I put a sheet of paper on the table in front of me and, pen in hand, began writing in a trance, the name of the one for whom I had written *Sunehere* "Sahir, Sahir..." I had completely filled the sheet with that name. (*The Revenue Stamp* 15)

Amrita describes her first meeting with Sahir, one small incident at a small town named Preet Nagar during adolescence that made him the daring darling of her heart:

> Between Lahore and Amritsar existed a small town—Preet Nagar, where once an evening of Urdu-Punjabi poetry was celebrated, and returning from here to Lahore, one had to walk down a stretch of two-three miles to catch a bus. The evening before, it had become cloudy and started pouring, but on the way back it was softly sunny. The muddy path was totally wet with the night-shower, at places it was messy. There were around fifteen people, walking ahead and behind, among whom was the one I had been observing since last night. *He just maintained silence—wherever his thin and tall shadow fell, I would quietly start walking in that shadow.... Well, it was just an incident, and in my conscious mind I had never ever contemplated that in all the years to come I would have to walk along this shadow....* (*Shadows of Words* 19; italics mine)

Amrita confesses that this meeting, this dream "created a beautiful, exotic vision — I often visualized a river, which had a boat, saw myself in that boat and him too" (*Shadows of Words* 19-20). This romantic dream cannot be realized in concrete terms but pierces her heart, "I love one man, but lost him twice" (*Shadows* 35). Out of several reminiscences which flash upon her eyes, the one which is striking is as follows:

> *Whenever Sahir came to see me in Lahore, it was as if he had somehow been conjured up by my silences. He had become so much a part of them, still still in the chair until it was time for him to go away...!*

> He would quietly go on chain-smoking...he would smoke half a cigarette, stub it out, and light another. When he was gone, the place was littered with cigarette ends....
>
> Sometimes, I intensely longed to touch him but I could not overcome my own reservations.
>
> It was a time when I lived in my imagination a great deal. When he was done, I would collect the stubs and preserve them secretly in a little cupboard. And then I would salvage them one by one and quietly sit and light them, one after the other.... I would feel the touch of his fingers by holding the stubs he once held... ! (*The Revenue Stamp* 110; italics mine)

One can guess the depth of sorrow in these lines. Throughout *Rasidi Ticket* Amrita sings of sorrow. However, this is not merely the song of sorrow but also of delight, redounding, as it does, to the glory of human nature. Suffering is the touchstone of the innate goodness of the human nature, even when this suffering befalls persons quite pure and innocent. The pain that she experiences is unbearably pathetic and it has been expressed by her through the immortal lines of Oscar Wilde:

> I determined to commit suicide. After a time that evil mood passed away, and I made up my mind to live, but to wear gloom as a king wears purple: never to smile again: to turn whatever house I entered into a house mourning: to make my friends walk slowly in sadness with me....
>
> Some people advised me to forget all this. It was ruinous advice. I would mean—the beauty of the sun and the moon, the music of daybreak and the silence of great nights, the rain falling through the leaves or the dew—creeping over the grass and making it silver—would all be tainted for me...to deny one's experience is to put a life into the lips of one's own life. It is no less than the denial of the soul. (*The Revenue Stamp* 34)

Bharat Muni, the reputed founder of the ancient Indian theatre, in his monumental work on dramaturgy, known as *The Natya Shastra*, has made a distinction between the feelings of life and the emotions of art. The former may be painful, but as they are manifested in a work of art they become capable of yielding delight. Her reflections on tragedy of life are exceedingly remarkable:

> Tragedy is, when the silver plating peels off and the contents of the bowl turn poisonous and penetrate into your imagination....
>
> Tragedy is, when you write your life's letter to your love and you yourself go and lose his address....
>
> Tragedy is, when with solely bleeding feet you stand where no pathway opens before you.... (*The Revenue Stamp* 36)

Amrita's autobiographies are a brilliant piece of a work of art. As a work of art it presents a world which has a strong semblance of the real life, but is essentially unlike it, because in this world things are logical, orderly and intelligible, bound as they are by the law of cause and effect or of probability or necessity. The result is a sort of 'distancing' where the world of realities is viewed not closely but at a distance. In this process the interested specters slowly rise above their personal limitations and prejudices, their selfish intents and concerns and contemplate on the human struggle against the odds of a life in a mood of entranced detachment. Amrita's meditative posture has been well described when she reflects on the essence of life:

> During the first phase, like a *Bodhisatva,* I sat looking upon everything with an eye of a wonder, the minutes were somehow magnified, though for no reason that I can explain.
>
> By the second, I had developed an overwhelming consciousness—it was the vigour of youth in revolt against the bastions of social tradition. The hatred and wrath rising up in me was like the precious stone in a toad's head.
>
> The third one was the courage to forget and demolish the present and to build a new future, the courage to shuffle dreams like cards before they are dealt out...the courage to take the losses in a game and to shuffle the cards again and deal them out afresh in the hope that luck would change.
>
> The fourth is this sense of isolation. (*The Revenue Stamp* 40)

The most powerful evidence of Amrita Pritam's confessional strain that brings to the fore her unspoken ordeal is evident in the passages dealing with the delicate human relationship, her unrequited love. Love, the first need of nature, the first prayer of heart, becomes the first martyr to this unspoken ordeal before it gets kindled and finds expression in words. If the language of love is silence, Amrita bears the pangs of separation with Sahir with stoical fortitude. She is quite open in telling about her illicit relationship with Sahir outside the laws of wedlock. At that time she was engaged to Imroz, but her physical relationship with Sahir was an ecstatic experience, "Strange meeting after many years when two lives throbbed like a poem" (*The Revenue Stamp* 116). It is not the guilt emanating from the hot heat of sexual passion that pains her but something else:

> A couple of years ago I met Sahir. The pressure he put on me was so great that I could not but go and stay with him for two days.... But my guilt lay in the green years of my youth. And though I wrote poems like 'Janam Jali' on this professed "guilt". I could still say with composure: "And are our guilt's heinous?" (*The Revenue Stamp* 116)

This confession exudes a quiet courage with which Amrita Pritam faced the tormenting pain and desolation she suffered. It shows her rare sensitivity, intensity and passion. Hidden secrets of relations with the opposite sex, and twisting of the soul in unbearable pain throws ample light on the lot of the fellow sufferers on highway to love: "when I made love/ eyes saw him/ and my ears heard him;/ my arms grow beautiful/ in the coupling/ and grow lean/ as they come away./ what shall I make of this?" This sentiment echoes in the following lines: "Love put it's thumb impression/ On the page of life./ But who'll settle the debt?" (*The Revenue Stamp* 77)

She is pale with longing for him. Casting off all shame and oblivious of all scandals she seizes on every possible pretext and tries to meet him. The pain of this love smitten lady cannot be diagnosed as it is in her heart that has been afflicted. It is the name of Sahir that has wounded her, "the sweetness of his lips is a pot of nectar,/ that's the only curd for which I crave." In the day she had no hunger, at night she is restless and cannot sleep. Leaving these troubles behind, she goes to the other side, "A hidden knowledge has taken hold of me". Then the pen in the hand, created a sensation on paper like "the leaves from the trees". Having taken up this bundle of suffering, the body, how can she throw it away? It belongs to Sahir, she is true to him and there is nothing to be ashamed of him:

> The relationship of mine with Sahir Ludhianvi, cannot be defined within the confines of a relationship.... Sitting among the ruins, at times in the valley of flowers—those moments came which cannot be defined in terms of relationship. There were no bodies in that relationship, only the heart, whose beat was heard somewhat by the earth and somewhat by the sky.... My relationship with Sahir can be somewhat identified in this light. In that long relationship over the years, it was only the heart—which was beating through the verses.... (*Shadows of Words* 20)

Apart from bringing to the fore hidden turmoil inside her body the said expression also is a reflection of social constraints that a woman had to face in giving vent to her purely personal and private experiences. The intensity of Amrita's devotion to Sahir and her courage in resisting every pressure to deviate from her chosen way of life can be demonstrated when we see her crazy love for Sahir. When her first baby was born and when she first looked upon his face, "it was the face of Sahir in mind..." (*The Revenue Stamp* 108). She says that she was merely feeding her frustration, "Like divinity aiming at the creation of a wonderful one.../ Free from the claims of the flesh.../ Free from all that flesh and blood has been heir to/ From the dawn of creation..." (*The Revenue Stamp* 108). At the same time, she confesses that she did it because:

> I had read about how a child develops and how his mind is shaped by his mother's thoughts.... My imagination drew me away from the world around me and I said to myself: if you always have Sahir's face in mind's eye, he'll grow to resemble him. (*The Revenue Stamp* 108)

Amrita's love for Sahir is reminiscent of a Sufi poet of Punjab, Mirza, who having seen the bewitching, exquisite and matchless beauty of Sahiba exclaimed with delight, "Man Mirza tan Sahiba". It means, when Mirza meets a beautiful girl, Sahiba, she feels that Mirza is a mind who has made her body his abode. In similar way, when Amrita describes her love for Sahir, it seems that Sahir has made her heart his abode; the bodies of Amrita and Sahir have become like holy shrines, where even the sternest puritans have come to learn about love. In her passionate description one can experience the union of two souls, not two bodies. And in this supreme meeting one experiences within the limits of the bodies the super consciousness which can make it boundless.

Why has love found this place in life? Amrita has found the answer to that mystery when these bodies of flesh and blood become a temple where, arising from within, the fragrance of incense offered in prayer begins, "Because a drop of your love got mixed in my cup/ I could drink the bitters of life...." (*The Revenue Stamp* 45)

WORKS CITED

De, Shobha. *Selective Memory.* New Delhi: Penguin, 1988.

Pritam, Amrita. *Rasidi Ticket.* Delhi: Hind Pocket Books, 1998.

——. *Shadows of Words.* Trans. Jyoti Sabharwal. Delhi: Macmillan, 1997.

——. *The Revenue Stamp.* Trans. Krishna Gorowara. Delhi: Vikas, 1998, Tharu, Su.

4

Comments on Amrita Pritam's *Magnum Opus*: The Skeleton

JAGDEV SINGH

In any internecine war or hostility, it is the innocent non-partisan who pays the highest price. The writings by women authors on holocaust of partition reflect the non-partisan point of view—of women and children struggling to keep alive in a hell let loose by their men-folk. Though few in number, the writing by women and children struggling are significantly rich in feeling and craftsmanship and exhibit a refinement and sensibility which are essentially feminine. *Sunlight on a Broken Column* (1961) by Indian-English novelist Attia Hosain, *Shadows of Time* (1987) and *The Heart Divided* (1957) by Pakistani novelists Meh Nigar Masroor and Mumtaz Shah Nawaaz respectively, *Ice-Candy-Man* (1988) by Bapsi Sidhwa, a Parsee and Pakistani expatriate settled in U.S. and *What the Body Remembers* (1999) by Shauna Singh Baldwin, an Indian expatriate settled in Canada are a few novels on the Partition written in English.

Similarly, *Mere Bhi Sanam Khane* (1949), *Aag Ka Darya* (1959) and *Akir-I-Shah Ke Hamsafar* (1979) by eminent novelist Qurratulain Hyder portray different aspect of the cataclysmic event in Urdu. While Krishna Sobti's masterpiece *Zindginama* (1979) presents pre-Partition scene in Hindi, *Epar Ganga Opar Ganga* (1947) by Jyotrimoyee Devi is a searing commentary on Partition in Bengali. All these novelists passionately record the longings, loses and compromises of their characters' simple lives, and the inherent consequence they face straddled between different cultures and religions.

Amrita Pritam[1] (b. 1919) is one such prolific woman-writer whose individual contribution to the gamut of Partition literature in Punjabi language is singular and far greater than that of any other woman writer. Amrita herself experienced the trauma that people suffered during those fateful days. Her poem *Aj Akhan Waris Shah Nu* (I Say Unto Waris Shah) is a heart-rending verse composed during those riot-torn days. Written as an invocation to Waris Shah, the most popular poet of Punjabi in the 18th century, it sought to articulate, through figural connection with *Heer*, the heroine of Waris Shah's masterpiece, the suffering which the womankind had to undergo in the course of this holocaust in the Punjab. With this cry from wounded soul, Amrita Pritam registered so much reception and exercised so rueful effect that on its score alone, she came to be known on either side of the Indo-Pak border as the "Voice of the Punjab".

The tragedy of Partition which, among other indignities and humiliations, involved a traumatic violation of womankind on a horrendous scale, furnished the objective correlative for Amrita's feminine concerns in her novels on the Partition theme. Attar Singh, an eminent critic of Punjabi literature, rightly comments: "Amrita Pritam's writings on the Partition riots are the most forceful. She has projected the violence against women in a heart-rending manner".[2] Out of a score of Amrita's novels, the Partition theme finds expression in only two of her novels: *Doctor Dev* and *Pinjar*. In *Doctor Dev*[3] (1949), there are indirect references to communal riots and violence and that too in the last part of the novel, but in *Pinjar* Amrita deals explicitly with the dislocation and violence against women during the Partition holocaust. On account of the limitations of space, here I focus exclusively on Amrita Pritam's novel, *Pinjar*[4] (1956).

The violations of womankind included dislocation and violence against women. The dislocation for women was even more traumatic than it was for men. The abducted women were dislocated from their natal families. Thus, their links with their parental homes and families were broken and the support, physical and emotional, that women do get from their natal home even after they enter their marital status, was also broken. Women were thus dislocated at two levels from the home and from the family.

The overwhelming memory and perception of Partition is

the relentless violence that accompanied the 'great divide'. The violence[5] directed against women took on additional forms, most of them located in sexuality. It included the molestation and rape done by the members of one community to women of the other, disfiguring of women by their limbs being hacked; parading of naked women in the form of processions; killing of women by their male kin in order to "save their honour"; encouraging women to commit suicide to avoid dishonour: "sacrificing" of women for the safety of males of the family and abduction of women during raids on the refugees caravans of during communal riots. In *Pinjar* Amrita Pritam has highlighted these two aspects of Partition—dislocation and violence—in great detail.

The locale of this novel is *Chatoani, Rattowal* and the surrounding villages in Gujarat district of Pakistani Punjab. The story covers a period of just more than a decade *i.e.* from 1935 to 1947.

Before Partition, a family of Hindu moneylenders lived in village *Chatoani.* A young girl of the family named Puro was engaged to another rich Hindu moneylender's son, Ram Chand, of a neighbouring village *Rattowal.* In the meantime British India is partitioned and both these villages fall in Pakistan territory.

Amrita Pritam beautifully portrays how a political decision of partitioning Punjab changes the equation of Hindu-Muslim relations in the area. Before Partition, the Hindu moneylenders dominated the Muslim population of these villages, but now they feel helpless and demoralized. The law and order situation deteriorates and a Muslim youth, Rashida of *Rattowal* village, abducts Puro when she had gone out in fields to get vegetables. Amrita tries to juxtapose the situation before and after the Partition. During pre-Partition days the Hindu moneylenders had abducted a Muslim girl of Rashida's family. At that time the Muslims were helpless, but now this area being Pakistan had emboldened the Muslims to abduct a Hindu girl in retaliation.

Thus abduction and rape of the women of one community by the men of the other was a way of 'dishonouring' the other community as real and symbolic subjugation. Inherent in these acts are also the notions of women as property. In both cases, Amrita highlights, it is the women that suffer the humiliation. When law and order deteriorated further, these abductions reached such a scale that the State Governments on both sides of the border were compelled to negotiate an agreement to recover abducted women.

One night Puro escapes from Rashida's confinement and manages to return to her family, but her parents shun her. Her father does not accept her and says, "Dear daughter, it is your fate! We are helpless." That it is the social stigma of abduction that is responsible for Puro's ostracisation is clear from her mother's comments: "Who will marry you now? You are defiled! Your religion is polluted" (28). Amrita tries to highlight that women had to constantly prove their innocence and assert their right to dignity in our patriarchal society.

In addition to the stigma associated with abduction, the other reason for not accepting the abducted women was the safety of the other members of the family. It points to the instances of men being bartered for the safety of the male members of the family during those harrowing days. Usually it was a daughter who was "sacrificed" or other young kinswomen. The reaction of Puro's mother makes this contention amply clear: "... Where will we keep you? Please go away at once. The Muslims will follow you. They will kill your father and brother" (28).

Such decisions were rationalized with the concept that daughters are in their natal homes only on a temporary basis and that they most eventually leave for their "real" home, that is the marital home.

When her parents did not accept her, Puro was obliged to go back. Rashida met her on the way and married her the very next day.

As the partition was based on the "two nation" theory of the Muslim League, the Hindu and Sikh population migrated towards East Punjab, while the Muslims shifted to the Western side of the Radcliff Line. Sometimes the caravans were miles long. Young girls of the opposite community were abducted by marauders during attacks on the caravans of migrating refugees. Ram Chand narrates one such attack in which his sister Lajo was abducted:

> As I started from my home with my aged mother on my back and joined the caravan, Lajo followed me. But after some time, she was missing.... (95)

Another form of violence against women portrayed in *Pinjar* is the parading naked women through the villages and towns. In the West Punjab, the Muslim hooligans abducted Hindu/ Sikh women and paraded them naked in the streets, while the Sikhs and Hindu did the same to Muslim women in East Punjab that fell in Indian Territory. Amrita mentions one such incident in village *Rattowal* itself, where a young girl was paraded naked: "One day Puro saw that a young girl was paraded naked while about ten youths in the form of a procession accompanied by a drummer passed by their village...." (91)

There are numerous instances of such processions in Partition literature written in other languages as well. But what distinguishes Amrita's account from those of other male writers is the feminine approach that Amrita follows in her novel. Chaman Nahal describes such a procession in his novel *Azadi* in the following words:

> The procession arrived. Arun counted them. There were forty women, marching tow abreast. Their ages varied from sixteen to thirty, although, to add to the grotesqueness of the display, there were two women, marching right at the end of the column, who must have been over sixty. They were all stark naked. Their heads were completely shaven: so were their armpits. So were their public regions.... Only the breasts and the hips gave away the age....[6]

The description of the funeral procession of decency in *Azadi* and the one portrayed by Amrita in *Pinjar* is indicative of her feminine angle to look at the event.

Amrita has highlighted that the cases of molestation and rape of women were not stray instances but were large-scale happenings. These happened not only during attacks on caravans of refugees but also in refugee camps protected by military guards. She points out one such instance in following words:

> There was a refugee camp in the adjoining village set up

> for the Hindus and Sikhs. The camp was guarded by the Military. But daily the Muslim hooligans would come and take away young girls from the camp at night and bring them back next morning. (91-92)

All these details depict the gruesome violence against women during those days. They were abducted, subjected to mass rape, at times in public places and in the presence of large gatherings. The rape was followed by other atrocities, chopping off the breasts, and even death. Many of the pregnant women had their wombs torn open. The survivors were retained for repeated rapes and humiliations until they were parceled out to decrepit wrecks, the aged, the leftovers who could not find a wife. In the meantime more women were abducted and the cycle was repeated all over again.

Puro accepts her fate and lives with Rashida and even bears him a son. But unlike Kulwant Singh Virk's heroine in his story *Khabbal* (Perennial Grass) as abducted Sikh woman, who tries to settle his sister-in-law in a Muslim family in Pakistan so that she has some kinship to sustain her in alien land, Puro makes efforts to send back her sister-in-law, Lajo, to her parents. Puro regrets that she was not accepted by her parents after her abduction, but helps Lajo to join her family. She justifies Lajo's recovery saying:

> The abductions have taken place on such a large scale that the parents have started accepting their daughters abducted by the opposite community. Rashida says that the Muslim girls are also recovered from India. Such of the recovered girls are with the offspring. (120)

When Puro's brother asked her to go to India, she prefers to stay back with her husband and children in Pakistan. Through Puro's refusal to return to India Amrita holds the primary leitmotif of estrangement and rape in counterpoint by the secondary motif of new horizon of hope in the form of a stronger marital bond as a source of sustenance for her.

The fiction on the Pakistan written in English and regional languages portraying the pulse of pulsating rural India shows the inseparable bonds of friendship between the two communities in the villages where the composite culture of India breathes in all its vitality. The shared cultural life encompasses the close friendly ties fostered by the cohesive social structure of villages even in the communally surcharged atmosphere.

Interestingly, there is no hostility between the two communities of the same village but against "outsiders". These outsiders come either as refugees, groaning with the agony of humiliations they have undergone, or as bands of marauders. The abiding relationship between Bhai Meet Singh, the Sikh priest of *Manomajra* and Imam Baksh, the Muslim priest of the same village in Khushwant Singh's *Train to Pakistan*, and the steadfast relationship between Sohne Shah, the Sikh headman of village Dhamyal and Allahditta, a Muslim of that village, in K.S. Duggal's *Naun te Mass* (Twice Born Twice Dead) show the harmony between the two communities of the same village.[7] But contrasted with it, Allahditta of village *Rattowal* in Amrita's novel *Pinjar* is shown abducting Lajo of the same village. This is not in line with the relations between different communities of the *same* village reflected in fiction on the theme.

Communal violence among the Hindus, Sikhs and the Muslims was not only due to mutual hatred among the communities for historical and religious reasons, there were other factors responsible for the bloodshed. The psychoanalyst Sudhir Kakar, holds sociological reason responsible for the violence:

> On a more sociological level, the chief reason for the preponderance of specifically sexual violence in the Partition riots in the north is that, as compared to many other parts of the country, the undivided Punjab was (and continue to be) a rather violent society. Its high murder rate is only one indication of a cultural endorsement of the use of physical force to attain socially approved ends such as the defence of one's land or of personal and family honour. There is now empirical evidence to suggest that the greater the legitimization of violence in some approved areas of life, the more is the likelihood that force will also be used in other sphere where it may not be approved. It is then quite understandable that sexual violence during the Partition riots could reach levels of brutality which have

been rarely been approached in subsequent riots in other parts of the country.[8]

Pinjar is the women's cry in prose against her existential fate and social abuse. Amrita's own spousal despair helped her to fashion complex metaphors to orchestrate the multiple agonies of her woman.... For its successful portrayal of pain and suffering of women who were used as pawns in the vendetta game during partition, Pinjar has been rightly chosen for a screen adaptation.

REFERENCES

1. Besides 18 volumes of verse, Amrita Pritam has to her credit 24 novels, 15 collections of short stories and 23 volumes of prose. Her autobiography *Rasidi Ticket* (Revenue Stamp, 1976) was an instant success because of her candour and intellectual integrity. Amrita Pritam was given Sahitya Akademi Award in 1966 for her collection of poetry *Sunehure* (messages). Her other distinction include the Award of *Padma Shri* in 1968, and conferment of the D.Litt. Degree on (*honoris cause)* by the University of Delhi in 1973. Amrita received the Jnanpith Award in 1982 for her *Kagaj ke Kanvas.*
2. Attar Singh. 1959. *Kavya Adhyayan.* Ludhiana: Lahore Book Shop, 86.
3. Amrita Pritam. 1969. *Dr. Dev.* Delhi: Navyug Publishers.
4. Amrita Pritam. 1996. *Pinjar.* Delhi: Aarsee Publishers. (All quotations with internal paging are from this edition of the novel. The writer of this paper has himself rendered them into English.)
5. Violence against women during Partition has been discussed in detail by Nighat Said Khan in "Identity, violence and women: a reflection on the partition of India 1947" in *Locating the Self. Perspectives on Women and Multiple Identity,* ed. Negha Said Khan, Rubina Saigal, Afiya Shehrbano Zia. Lahore: ASR Publications, 1994. 163.
6. Chaman Nahal. 1975. *Azadi.* New Delhi: Orient Paperbacks.
7. The writer of the paper has discussed this aspect in his book *Bonds and Borders: A Study of Communal Conflict and Concord in Indo-Pak Fiction.* 1996. Delhi: Ajanta Publications. 12.
8. Sudhir Kakar. 1996. *The Colours of Violence.* New Delhi: Penguin Books. 38.

5

PARTITION: THE OTHER SIDE QURRATULAIN HYDER'S *FIREFLIES IN THE MIST*

M.P. SINHA

India's partition in 1947 and the holocaust that followed it made every sensible Indian feel that it was a grave blunder to divide this ancient country on the grounds of religion. Few at that time could realise that the division was the creation of the people who had vested interests.

Most of the novels written on the theme of partition lay emphasis on the bloodshed and suffering of the innocent people and tenderness of humanity in the times of brutality. Qurratulain Hyder's *Fireflies in the Mist* is a different kind of novel. As there was less bloodshed on the eastern side, she is more concerned with the causes that led to partition and the misery, civil war, frustration and anguish that followed it on both the sides—East Bengal and West Bengal—even after the creation of Bangladesh. Mikhail Bakhtin, after analyzing Dostoevsky's novels, arrives at the conclusion that they are on a new polyphonic type of fiction in which a variety of discourses expressing different ideological positions are set in play without being ultimately placed and judged by a totalising authorial discourse. *Fireflies in the Mist* follows Dostoevsky's tradition; the different ideologies are juxtaposed together without any authorial discourse and the reader is left at liberty to choose one or reject all. Aamer Hussein in his review of the novel writes:

> Never bound to a single ideology or perspective, Hyder articulates one viewpoint only to contradict it in another voice.[1]

1. Printed on the back cover of the novel. All quotations are from *Fireflies in the Mist*. New Delhi : Sterling Publishers, 1996.

The novel begins with a detailed description of Dacca and its important inhabitants. The families described are European, Eurasian and Indian (Hindu, Muslim and Christian). However, the greater focus is on the Sarkar, The Zaman Chowdhri, the Roy, the Bannerjee and the Barlow families.

The house Caledonia built by a Scotsman called MacDonnel Saheb is bought by Romesh Chandra Sarkar when the third generation of MacDonnell Saheb leave Dacca for ever and finally settle in Calcutta. Romesh Chandra Sarkar renames it Chandrakunj. Soon after his entrance into the house an incident changes the whole course of his life. It so happens that Romesh Baboo's coachman's child, Abdul Qadir, finds a photo album while cleaning Augur MacDonnell's landau. It is a morocco-bound, gold-rimmed volume containing small photographs in sepia. The photographs are of the important English officers, landlords and Nawabs of India. He takes the album to Sir Nurul Zaman Chowdhri. Sir Nurul tells him that their owner is Syed Ahmed Ali, Nawab of Chitpur. After this first acquaintance, a relationship starts between the two families and later is firmly established in the form of friendship between Sir Nurul's younger brother Fakhrul Zaman Chowdhri and Romesh Chandra Sarkar as both are lovers of music and theatre. The friendship between Romesh Baboo and Fakhrul Zaman Chowdhri continues till the untimely death of the nawabzada. In maintaining a high standard of living Romesh Baboo loses almost all his property. His first son Benoy Sarkar graduates from Calcutta in medicine. But being a benevolent and large hearted person he takes no fees from the poor and thus earns very little. His wife dies early leaving behind her daughter Deepali Sarkar and two sons. Benoy Sarkar's young brother Dinesh Sarkar is hanged by the British government for his revolutionary activities.

Sir Nurul's only heir is Qamrul Zaman Chowdhri who is unhappily married to a woman whom he never loved. In fact, he was almost betrothed to Maliha, Fakhrul's daughter but as Fakhrul dies almost bankrupt, Qamrul's mother insisted on his marriage to a wealthy family for a good dowry. Frustration in love and Maliha's marriage to a Maulvi drives Qamrul to devote most of his time to library and politics. Maliha's husband, Maulvi Burhan Ahmed, a self-respecting preacher lives according to the strict principles of Islam. As he is a poor man and does not accept anything from his wife's side, he lives hand to mouth. Maliha forgets her rich past, lives as a faithful wife and gives birth to Rehan Ahmed, the most important male character in the novel. Nawab Qamrul Zaman Chowdhri out of his love for Maliha wants to get his daughter Jehan Ara married to Rehan Ahmed but the clash of principles comes in the way, although Rehan and Jehan Ara love each other.

The third family is of Rev. Paul Matthew Bannerjee, his wife Giribala Esther Bannerjee and their daughter Rosie. Giribala a widow Brahmin is saved by Sir Nurul and married to the newly convert Paul Matthew Bannerjee. Rev. Bannerjee, like Maulvi Burhan Ahmed, remains loyal to his new faith throughout his life, rather foolishly. When Rosie marries Basant Sanyal, he deserts her forever and prays to God to save her soul.

The fourth is the Roy family of the Woodland. The Roys are rich and highly educated and loyal to the British government. But as luck would have it Uma Roy comes in contact with revolutionaries in London School of Economics and returns to India as a communist. Although never in the forefront, she helps her comrades by all means.

The fifth is the Barlow family that has stayed in India for three generations, all I.C.S. officers. Charles Barlow, grandson of Sir Edward Barlow and son of James Barlow, is an unhappy man though he enjoys a high position in the government. He finds his family, illustrations in all ways, declining and decomposing slowly and resigns himself to fate.

All the families are introduced slowly and artistically and what is more remarkable is that two are Hindu families, one poor and the other rich, one is a rich Muslim family with poor relations and the rest two are Christian, one a poor Indian and the other a powerful and rich English. The opening page reminds us of *A Passage To India*, E.M. Forster describes the town Chandrapore on the bank of the Ganga and Qurratulain Hyder the city of Dacca on the same river. The difference between the two novelists is that whereas Forster fictionalises Bankipur (Patna) and the Barebar hills of Gaya into Chandrapore and Marabar hills, Hyder depicts Dacca and its port Narayanganj as they were in 1935. We can say that Forster tells history in the form of fiction but Hyder mixes fiction and history so meticulously that it is difficult for us to say which part of the novel is history and which one fiction.

After describing Dacca and the Padma, the novelist moves on to the history of the houses and their owners—Caledonia and MacDonnel Saheb, Chandrakunj and Romesh Chandra Sarkar, Lily Cottage and Matthew Bannerjee, Woodland and Sir Pritish Roy and Arjumand Manzil and Sir Nurul Zaman Chowdhri and his brother Nawabzada Fakhrul Zaman Chowdhri. Besides, the photographs in the houses lead us to the Victorian age and also the late Moghul period. Side by side is narration of the revolutionary activities. Then in a very natural way we are introduced to characters in action—Deepali Sarkar, Rosie Shrilha Bannerjee and Jehan Ara responding to the roll-call in the local college.

Rehan Ahmad, who inherits Virendra Nath Chattopadhyay's* characteristics, visits Deepali Sarkar's house. He sees Deepali's uncle's photograph in the drawing room, asks a few questions, discusses music and leaves the place. Deepali does not recognize him as he is in the guise of a *baul* singer but Rehan perceives the spirit of a revolutionary in her. Deepali is instantly entrusted with the task of acting as Kulsum ayah in the house of Charles Barlow, an I.C.S. officer, where the plan to nab the revolutionaries is to be discussed. For this, she has to contact Miss Uma Roy, a graduate from London School of Economics and lecturer in her college, who is a close associate of Rehan Ahmad. With the assistance of Uma Roy she acts her role well and saves the revolutionaries from surprise attack.

Rehan Ahmad, the moving spirit behind the communist movement finally appears before Deepali in his true form in a remote part of East Bengal. Anil Biswas, a comrade, gives Deepali the message that she is wanted by Rehan Ahmad for a secret meeting. She finds him really handsome, a true heart-winning youth. She learns from him that he did his B.A. from Aligarh Muslim University and then studied at London School of Economics where he met Uma Roy. He tells her about the

---

* Virendra Nath Chattopadhyay was Sarojini Naidu's brother. He turned a revolutionary.

political situation in England in the thirties, the left upsurge in the intellectuals, especially creative writers like Auden, Spender, MacNiece and Isherwood.

In the romantic greenery of Sunderbans Rehan Ahmad and Deepali live for a week and there Deepali gets enough time to study and understand Rehan's heart and mind. She begins to love him. Romance and revolution go together; a rationalist can never be bold and ready to play with dangers. Conscience makes cowards us of all, says *Hamlet*.

Deepali returns after her sojourn in the Sunderbans. There is the marriage of her friend's brother Nayyarul Zaman Choudhry. Jehan Ara asks her to bring reels from her room. While taking out the reels from the almirah she sees Rehan Ahmad's photograph with the words inscribed:

> To Jehan Ara Begum, the lady of my dreams,
> From Rehan Ahmad, London, April 16, 1936.

She is stunned. How could the man whom she adored and loved so deeply deceive her? He did not say anything when she talked about Jehan Ara when they were in the Sunderbans, she thinks. She leaves Arjumand Manzil, takes rest at home and then goes back to Shantiniketan to complete her studies. At night, she has a nightmare; all the past events reel before her eyes and all male figures are egg-shaped, sans eyes and ears.

Time passes. The Quit India Movement is launched on 9 August 1942. Deepali takes the party line to remain aloof from the movement because the British government is fighting against Italy's fascism and Germany's nazism. The Communist Party of India splits with the Congress and Rehan Ahmad and Deepali do not take part in the Quit India Movement. But the other members of the party consider these two to be cowards. Rosie, Mushir Masoodul and Jyoti take active part in the movement but, revolutionary as they are, they unheeded Gandhiji's principle of non-violence. Masoodul, Mushir and Jyoti are killed while bombing the government offices and Rosie is badly wounded when a bomb explodes. She is caught and arrested by the police. She is taken to jail and from there to a hospital for treatment. As she is a revolutionary, all patients admire her and secretly wish her to remain firm in her convictions. Her father, a devout Christian, loyal to England from the core of his heart, moves heaven and earth for her acquittal. He requests Charles Barlow for her release to no avail. Barlow's sister, a missionary, comes to the hospital to dissuade Rosie from revolutionary activities and beg pardon for her conduct. Rosie refuses to do so. As the luck would have it, Miss Barlow brings Robi Sanyal with her. Next time, Basant Sanyal, Robi Sanyal's brother, visits the hospital. He is enamoured with her looks and what is more being a nationalist himself, he feels naturally sympathetic to her. Rosie in her letter to Deepali writes:

> I think two things floored him: my looks and the courage of my convictions. (226)

Soon after her acquittal, she is married to Basant Sanyal and becomes Radhika. She accepts the change happily but her father abandons her and prays to God to save her soul!

Rehan and Uma Roy who remain neutral to the Quit India Movement discuss the current problems and national politics and in course of the conversation Rehan tells his own story—his relation with the late Fakhrul Zaman, the fate of his mother Maliha who was to be married to Qamrul Zaman Chowdhry, his own education, his betrothal to Jehan Ara and final break with her for the reason that he, a communist, would not make compromise with his principles. He tells that he asked Jehan Ara to go with him, leaving all her wealth and family behind but Jehan Ara, brought up in a Muslim aristocratic family, refused to do so. Now he wants to marry Deepali in whom he finds a real comrade, bold and intelligent and free from the prejudices of her class. We feel sympathy for him; he is honest to the core. If he wanted he could adopt the aristocratic ways of his maternal grandfather, Fakhrul Zaman Chowdhri, and be at the helm of the affairs of the Zaman Chowdhry Estate. Jehan Ara, being brought up as a Muslim aristocrat does not have the courage to leave her parents behind. Rehan narrates her reaction when he proposed for leaving the house stealthily:

> Suddenly, she broke down and cried. I was furious. I said, if you do not have the guts to defy your autocratic father, how will you fight in the revolution alongside your comrade husband?

> I was about to blurt out that I needed a brave girl, a real fighter, as my wife, and not a silly weakling like her. Better sense prevailed and I kept quiet. I lingered there another few minutes, hoping that she would agree to come away with me. She didn't. I left her there shedding copious tears, and returned to my room. At the break of dawn I went away from Arjumand Manzil for good. (205)

Uma Roy feels sympathy for him. Rehan says that she always reminds him of his mother. For his sake Uma Debi mixes with Dr. Benoy Sarkar so much so that people begin to gossip. She tells Dr. Sarkar about Deepali's sojourn in the Sunderbans with Rehan. Deepali's secret expedition to the Sunderbans shocks Dr. Sarkar but a progressive man that he is, he soon revives and says to Uma Debi next day:

> As a self-respecting, orthodox father I ought perhaps recall her forthwith from Shantiniketan, shut her up in a room, get hold of a Hindu lad and marry her off. I wouldn't do any of these things. (236)

When Uma Debi speaks of the weak points of Rehan Ahmad—his hand-to-mouth existence, his break with Jehan Ara Begum and the gloomy prospect of his practice after his daughter's marriage to a Muslim boy—Dr. Sarkar replies with a smile:

> I have lost my wife and brother. Both were young. They would have liked to live. I want people to be alive and happy. I do not believe in this nonsense of rebirth. One is born only once. One must not make others miserable in their short lives. If I am convinced that Deepali and Rehan are genuinely in love, I would certainly allow them to marry. Hindu society, my own medical practice, etc. are not more important than the personal happiness of my daughter. You ought to applaud my progressive views. (237)

Certainly Dr. Sarkar is more progressive than the people around him.

Jehan Ara suffers for her close adherence to tradition and timidity. Born and educated in the best of tradition of Muslim aristocracy she fails to act like Deepali and Rosie. She does not protest the unequal marriage with the grotesque Nawab who is twice her age. She remains a showpiece in the beginning and then a faithful housewife after the birth of her son Akmal.

After her husband's death she returns to Arjumand Manzil. She loses her son Akmal in the 1965 Indo-Pakistan war and meets her tragic end when the opposite group of Sheikh Mujibur Rehman kills the entire family. The scene is so ghastly that the only survivor, Mala, loses her speech. The one time teeming house is without a direct inheritor. The entire property now shifts to Rehan Ahmed who had been in Calcutta during the turbulent period. Nawab Chowdhri, the great advocate of partition, loses everything; the family line stops for ever.

Deepali, who shifted along with her father and brothers to the West Indies after India's partition and was happily married to Barrister Sen, comes to India and Bangladesh to attend the celebration of an anniversary of Yasmin, a great singer of Bangladesh, who had died in England. The irony of fate is that Yasmin lived an unhappy life, was a total failure in Europe and committed suicide there as she had nothing to hold on but the Bangladeshis glorify her as a true daughter of their country who best represented its culture abroad. Deepali, who has read her diary, knows the grim reality. She is embittered. The tragic end of Arjumand Manzil, the Barlow family, the desertion of the other houses, all caused by the partition make her sad. Divided India has no charm for her; it is a heavily mutilated country smeared with clotted blood. The novel ends with the sense of the loss of the glory that will never come back.

> She began to hum a Bengali hymn to Shankar and peeped out at the sparkling expanse of the sky and water, closed her eyes again. What should I meditate on? Can't concentrate on gods, have they failed? Broken down? (347)

The novel ends rather forcibly with a philosophic note:

> For millions of years the sun has been rising and going down and rising again and going down and rising.

The ending sentence reminds us of Yeats's "Lapis Lazuli" but the philosophic note rings too weakly to give us sustenance to bear the wound of partition.

The main theme of the novel is partition. But, what makes it great and different from other novels on the theme is that whereas other novels are confined to describing the holocaust which preceded and followed independence, Hyder opens our eyes to the loss the Indian people suffered and are still suffering.

Her main concern is the loss of a world where people lives in harmony despite their social and religious differences, spoke the same language, studied the same literature, maintained cultural unity and struggled unitedly for the liberation of their motherland. In a very subtle way she stresses the importance of the leftist organizations which tried to break the narrow, man-created artificial barriers of caste and religion.

The tenderness with which the idyllic beauty of Bengal is depicted is really heart-touching. It is an integral part of India and culturally bound with other parts. It is a province where *barahmasa* is sung, where the sailors sing *bhatiyali* in their boats and where *baul* singers roam from place to place; and where the revolutionary songs of Qazi Nazrul Islam and melodious songs of Rabindra Nath Tagore are sung by all people. The relationship between different houses—Arjumand Manzil, Chandrakunj, Woodland and Lily Cottage—is intimate and cordial and neither religion nor wealth stands as barrier between them. The Nawab is always ready to send poor persons like Dr. Sarkar and Rev. Bannerjee in his car. This is a world where everybody is loyal to the other and where everybody is overtly or covertly excepting Rev. Bannerjee, against the British rule.

The author's natural sympathy, which is "non-said", is with the revolutionaries—the fireflies in the mist. She does not touch Mahatma Gandhi and the Indian National Congress, a deliberate *difference* to use Jacques Derrida's term. She is critical of the Indian Muslim League, dominated by nawabs and big landlords, which divided the Indian people in two nations to serve the purposes of the rich. In Part II, Chapter 7 of the novel, Qamrul Zaman Chowdhri's preparation for a meeting of the League is described:

> A placard in Bengali which read Pakistan Is Our Birthright had been placed behind the chairs on the makeshift *dais*. Nawab Qamrul Zaman's only son and heir, Nayyarul Zaman, was overseeing the arrangements while humming a Tagore's song...oblivious to the inherent contradiction in the situation. (127)

Before entering the *Zanana* Deepali catches sight of the map of Pakistan which Nayyarul Zaman has pinned up on the wall, she stops and reads the caption:

> Punjab, Assam, Bengal, Kashmir, Sarhad (North-West Frontier Province), Sind, Baluchistan, P-A-K-I-S-T-A-N. (129)

Nawab Zaman Chowdhri sees her reading and asks her what she is reading. As the subject is political, a long discussion takes place between them. The discussion reveals the fact that both the All India Muslim League and the Indian National Congress are dominated by nawabs, rajahs and big landlords and it is their clash of interest that has led them to use religion as a weapon and divide the people into two nations. Zaman Chowdhri represents the All India Muslim League point of view and his bitterness is so intense that even Deepali gets impatient and cuts him short.

> "But, uncle", she cut in impatiently, "both communities started their revivalist movements and were encouraged by the...."

However, the nawab does not allow her to complete the sentence and wraps up the discussion rather rudely which is quite un-characteristic of him!

> British! I agree. Well, why did we let ourselves be manipulated by them? He collected his papers and carried them to the writing table. (136)

After his departure, Deepali hears a mystic Bengali lyric by Lalan Shah, which Rehan had sung for her in the Sunderbans. She remembers his words:

> In every country, the Sufis usually belonged to the working classes and led the masses against the autocracies of their times. In Bengal the Hindu Sanyasis and Madari fakirs had fought together against the Company's forces in 1767. He had proceeded to talk about Bengal's great singing Sufis...Shaikh Madan Baul, Shatolan Shah, Hasan Raza, Lalan Shah, whose lyrics had inspired Tagore's poetry and music. (137)

The ideological division is clear cut: One ideology is for the landlords and the other for the working class. Rehan and Deepali support the cause of the working class and hence work for united India but people like Qamrul Zaman Chowdhri for the division of the nation for their own benefit. In the misty atmosphere created by the British government and spread and intensified by the landlords, Rehan, Deepali, Rosie, Mushir, Anil, Masoodul and Jyoti create light like fireflies to show the Indian people the real path.

It is typical of Hyder, in contrast to Bernard Shaw, to make a number of characters speak the same ideology. The communist or Marxist ideas come to the reader not only through Rehan and Deepali but also through Rosie, Mushir, Masoodul and Jyoti. Rosie learns in her college:

> ... how Ireland's Sinn Fein, Russia's Social Democrats and Mazzine's young Italy had influenced Indian radicals. The terrorists had said: We know we can't get freedom by killing a few Englishmen. We only wish to prove our rulers that we have guts to kill and get killed. (56-57)

We are told that the women of Bengal were not far behind in revolutionary activities: Kalpana Dutt attacked government armours in Chittagong on 30 April 1930, Pritilata Wadedar bombed the European Club in Chittagong and Shanti and Sumiti were deported to the Andaman and Nicobar Islands as life prisoner for killing the English District Magistrate of Comilla and Beena Das shot at the Governor of Bengal.

After joining the communist party Rosie learns many new things in the study group. Earlier she had a false notion about the Muslims that they were womanisers, fanatics and toadies. Mushir breaks her prejudice and counts the names of the revolutionaries like Khudadad Khan, Hyder Raza, Zafar Ali (the London-based radicals), Zafar Ali, Mirza Abbas, Ali Ahmed Siddique, Mujtaba Hussain, Syed Rahmat Ali Shah, Cassim Mansur and Ashafaqullah Khan. Mushir in his long speech concludes:

> Historically and culturally I am [a Muslim]. Look the trouble is when a Hindu glories in his tradition it is Indian culture and Indian philosophy, when a Muslim mentions his own heritage he is a communalist. We must correct this attitude before it is too late. Or else the country will break up after the British leave. (59)

Although Mushir is right in his conclusion, he is off the point when he says that he is culturally a Muslim. In fact religion is a component of culture. The Buddhists of Japan, for example, are culturally different from those of India and so are the Muslims of Indonesia from those of the Arab countries.

The discussions in the study group make her revise her past opinions and think of India as a nation where people despite differences in religion are all united and this unity has been strengthened by the revolutionaries and, that a large number of revolutionaries are from the Muslim community. She learns the history of Ghadar Party founded by Maulana Barkatullah and his comrades in America and the setting up of the Government of Free India by him in Kabul in 1916. Jyoti, the bespectacled comrade, counts the names of the Indian Muslims who became communist leaders—Ferozuddin, Mansur, Fazal Ilahi, Qurban Shaukat Usmani, Mian Azal Shah and Ahmad Amir Khan. The Sikh revolutionary Sardar Ajit Singh disguised himself as a Russian Muslim and called himself Mirza Hasan Khanov and Sarojini Naidu's brother Birendra Nath Chattopadhyay who carried a price of ten thousand rupees on his head was a polyglot and could disguise himself in many ways. He counts a few more names who were born Hindus but assumed Muslim names for the sake of safety. In other words, the Hindu Muslim distinction was meaningless for them; they were Hindu and Muslim at the same time, did pray in a temple and attend *namaj* in a masjid.

During the Quit India movement, the group splits. Rehan and Deepali follow the party line but Rosie, Mushir, Masoodul and Jyoti follow the line of the nationalist revolutionaries. Jyoti, Mushir and Masoodul are killed while attacking a police station and Rosie is badly injured. Qamrul Zaman Chowdhri leads the Indian Muslim League. Independence is gained in 1947 but before it the nation is divided. The British government and the aristocracy become successful in executing their plan. The working class is betrayed. The message is: religion serves the interests of the rich, the ruling class.

The novel does not end here. Divided India is presented in the final chapters of the novel. Deepali who has emigrated to the West Indies comes back and sees the mutilated nation. She visits Arjumand Manzil, now inherited by Rehan Ahmad and his wife Johra. She goes to the playhouse. She is lost in a reverie. This reverie is continual and so the past and the present mingle here. In fact, the playhouse is a symbol of the past glory. The cultural unity that existed in the past is no more. While reading this chapter we are reminded of Yeats's poem "The Circus Animals' Desertion." Qamrul Zaman Chowdhri would never have thought of the dangerous consequences of Muslim fanaticism. He led the people of East Bengal and the rest of India for the division of the nation on religious grounds and the same Muslims (the Bangladeshis) annihilated his entire family.

At the end of the chapter "The Playhouse", Deepali's reverie is broken by Rehan's arrival. Deepali is angry with him. Rehan did not marry Jehan Ara because she was a rich woman but, now, he is wallowing in Qamrul Zaman Chowdhri's wealth. Where is his communism and where are his revolutionary ideas? She accuses him of living a double life, covertly:

> So Ronu. Most of us lead double life. You are not Mlle Marie nor Mlle Yvonne. You are the Negro cook who carries their canvas bag. You are also *involved*.

Rehan retorts her and says that she too has deserted the path. He asks:

> After you migrated to the West Indies, shouldn't you have organized a trade union movement and worked for the red revolution among the plantation labourers?
>
> A little later he speaks philosophically:
>
> You see Deepali, to keep the lamp burning requires a great quantity of oil. And the trouble is that sometimes the oil runs out pretty soon. Now you have become a ringside spectator. You have your own sympathy for the downtrodden. You hate injustices and wars. But you are no longer in the actual arena. To remain consistently inside the spheres of misery and struggle, requires a hell of a lot of courage. Those who do so are considered eccentrics or plain fools. (323)

Deepali realises her mistake that she, too, has acted like Rehan. However, she says, but slowly with a feeling of defeat:

> But quite a few have not turned out to be cowardly like us.... There are many who have kept the lamp burning. (324)

Rehan agrees with her and then tells the biggest truth of partition:

> Yes, indeed. There are many who have kept the lamp burning. There are Hindu-Muslim riots in many states of India except Bengal. Why? Because of Bengal's strong Leftist tradition which was created by people like you and me. Some of us did fall off by the roadside, but many more are still there.... All luck to them. (324)

We can comment that Rehan and his comrades are feeble fireflies in the mist created by the opium of religion.

The forty-second chapter titled "Victorious Morning Star", English translation of Rehan's niece's name Nasira Najmas Sahas, leads us to the world of the seventies where we encounter the views of the younger generation of Bangladesh. Rehan, Deepali, Nasira and Furqan (Rehan's son) discuss the contemporary situation. Nasira is a firebrand girl of modern time and Furqan a pacifist. He is of the opinion that religion alone can save the world:

> Nasira Apa, the fact is that now Jesus Christ is my hero too, and Imam Hussain and his descendants—the Apostolic Imams, and the Sufis of Islam. They were the real original quietists. (328)

Nasira contradicts him sharply:

> The opium has affected you completely. Alas ... Peace spread by religion. Indeed! In the West army chaplains accompany their forces on either side of the battle line and pray to the same god for victory. In the Indo-Pak wars Hindu and Sikh soldiers carry the pictures of goddess Durga and Guru Gobind Singh and Pakistani forces raise the battle cry of God is Great, and invoke the help of Ali. Out here, in 1971, Islam raged on both sides of the war front. (328)

Then she asks if she would be allowed to speak about Yasmin. When Furqan remarks: "Ah! The celebrated daughter of Bangladesh", she gets angry and in one breath tells the truth about her and then comments:

> The maulvis did not forgive her for her waywardness. But thousands of Muslim girls were raped here during the War

> of Liberation, countless had to become street-walkers. Not a single maulvi of the Islamic world protested against the horrible situation. (329)

Deepali is embittered. She feels that the nation has been betrayed. When she is asked to speak in the meeting honouring Yasmin, she decides to speak the truth, although it would not be fit for the occasion. The speech, I take to be the message of the novel:

> The concept of Mother India has been given to the rest of the country by the terrorists of Bengal. They worshipped Divine Power in the image of Kali—the destroyer. They believed in the pre-historic Dravidian concept of the mother goddess. The British branded them as terrorists. Indians called them revolutionaries. Many among them were anti-Muslim as well. Bankim Chandra's novel *Anand Math* was their Bible. The cross-currents of the politics of Bengal's Bhadralog and Muslim gentry gave birth to East Pakistan, and the internal politics of West and East Pakistan created Bangladesh. Individual personality clashes and temperaments and actions of political leaders build or destroy nations. (332)

The novel ends with Deepali's musings. She is utterly frustrated. She, while returning in a plane to the West Indies where her permanent home is, begins to hum a Bengali song to Shankar and peeps out at the sparkling expanse of sky and water. Then she closes her eyes again and begins to question herself.

> What should I meditate on? Can't concentrate on gods, have they failed? Broken down? (347)

She then thinks of a hopeful future:

> There are many hidden pictures inside me. Which one shall I concentrate on? Which melody shall I sing? There are so many secret melodies inside. (347)

The novelist has built the structure artistically. The story covers roughly a period of one hundred years. It introduces first like a family genealogy, British and Indian people of the nineteenth century and then slowly moves on to the nineteen thirties when the revolutionaries of Bengal were most active. The largest part of the novel is devoted to their ideas and activities. It stops in the middle of the seventies to review the past objectively and reflect on the contemporary situation.

India's partition was catastrophic indeed. The feudal lords and the guardians of religion were the main forces behind partition and cultural disintegration. The war of Independence of Bangladesh in 1971 made it amply clear that the guardians of religion on both sides, West Pakistan and East Pakistan, prayed to Allah for their country's victory and forgot the fact that both sides were believers. One thing is clear: religion is opium in our age; it divides humanity. Differences must be wiped out. Rehan Ahmad says to Deepali:

> Kulsum—Deepali.... Some day, Baba, I'll explain to you how through communism, we can erase the senseless difference between Kulsum and Deepali. (113)

In the polyphony of discourses, Rehan's is the most prominent—sensible, rational and humane.

6

The Short Stories of Tagore: The Poems of Human Heart

B.G. TANDON

Pain is perhaps the most abiding condition of man's being. He is born in pain, he lives through pain, and he takes his last breath in pain. The mother suffers when the child is born. The seed bursts when the plant grows. The sight of a decrepit old man, a painfully sick man, and of a dead body made Gautam renounce the world. Pain is the charter of life and the sensitivity to the pain of others is compassion or *Karuna.* It distinguishes man from man, and it is this that elevates literature to scriptural greatness. The maneuvering of the story, the insight into human character, the power of thought, the splendour of language, and the laying bare of the atmosphere, are all laudable excellences, but the virtue that lends true potency to a work of literature is awareness of the pain that corrodes human heart: the compassion for man's suffering is the true test of both man and of the literature that he produces. It is this quality that marks the great scriptures of the world. It is this that makes literary works soulful and human and gives them the status of classics. And it is this that lies at the root of Tagore's pre-eminence as a man of letters. It is this that made Gandhi call him poet. His short stories are so many poems of the human heart.

For my first illustration I take 'The Postmaster', a touching story of unsaid sorrow. The plot is slight. A young postmaster, Nilkante, employed an orphan village girl of twelve or thirteen, Ratan, to do housework for him, taught her language, was nursed by her in his illness, and at last left her and the village where he had worked for ever. At the moment of parting this is what transpired between them:

'I'm leaving tomorrow, Ratan', said the postmaster.

'Where are you going, Dadababu ?'

'I'm going home.'

'When are you coming back ?'

'I shan't come back again.'

For several minutes neither of them spoke. Then the girl suddenly asked:

'Dadababu, will you take me home with you ?'

'How could I do that !' said the postmaster.

After a time, the postmaster said:

'I'll tell the man who replaces me that he should look after you as I have.'

The girl had meekly suffered many scolding from him in the past, but these kind and generous words she could not bear.

She cried, 'No, no, you mustn't say anything to anyone.'

At the departing moment, he gave her some extra money. But she fled, saying, 'Dadababu, I beg you, don't give me any money.'

"The postmaster felt a huge anguish: the image of a simple young village girl's grief-stricken face seemed to speak great inarticulate universal sorrow. He felt a deep desire to go back." But the boat moved and "he reflected philosophically that in life there are many separations, many deaths. What point was there in going back ? Who belonged to whom in this world ?"

"But Ratan had no such philosophy to console her.... A faint hope lingered in her mind that Dadababu might return."

Tagore comments: "O poor, unthinking human heart ! Error will not go away, logic and reason are slow to penetrate. We cling with both arms to false hope, refusing to believe the weightiest proofs against it, embracing it with all our strength. In the end it escapes, ripping our veins and draining our heart's blood; until, regaining consciousness, we rush to fall into snares of delusion all over again."

I now come to another extremely compassionate short story of Tagore, 'Unwanted'. It deals with a similar situation, only that the male-female roles are changed: the postmaster becomes an ailing woman, Kiran, and the orphan girl becomes the orphan boy, Nilkanta. At the time of parting she advised him to return to his village. He burst out crying. Here Tagore turns the key and dots the situation with an incident that unfolds the unspoken poetry of the human soul.

The postmaster was alone, but in this story Kiran had a full family and they had come to this village for a change of climate that might restore her to health. To them came her brother-in-law, Satish, who took away part of Kiran's attention from Nilkanta, and this smarted the possessor adolescent.

Satish had a fancy inkstand. The morning before their departure, it was nowhere to be found. He was sure that Nilkanta had stolen it. Taking him away, Kiran asked him, 'Nilu, if you have that inkstand, give it me quietly and no one will say anything to you'. His eyes swelled with tears, from which she concluded that he had not stolen the inkstand.

In the evening, Kiran opened the boy's box to put some parting gifts into it, and lo and behold, she found the inkstand in it.

Unnoticed by her, the boy saw everything and realised that he had been caught. How could he tell her that he had stolen the inkstand but he was not a thief? He had done it in retaliation and out of neglected love.

The next day there was no sign of the orphan boy. 'We must look at his box now,' said Kiran's husband 'Not on any account,' said she adamantly. Later, she took out the inkstand and secretly threw it into the Ganges.

Kiran and her family returned home, only Nilkanta's village dog remained. It wondered along by the river, forgetting to eat, searching, searching and waiting.

I may now recall another much anthologized short story, 'Holiday'. Here the central character is not an orphan, but a boy of thirteen or fourteen, Phatik, whom his widowed mother sent to his maternal uncle in Calcutta for better education. He was a nuisance at home, but in his uncle's house he met with such loveless indifference that he longed to return home and, in fact, asked his uncle one day: 'Uncle, when will I be going home to see my mother ?' 'When the school holiday comes,' said his uncle.

One night when rain poured relentlessly and he was in fever, he left his uncle's house and proceeded towards his home village; but they brought him back. His fever climbed alarmingly and in the delirious state he asked his uncle, 'Uncle, has my holiday-time come?'

The next day, the uncle said softly in his ear, 'Phatik, I've sent for your mother'.

Another day passed when his mother came bursting into loud wail of grief, she sobbed, 'Phatik, my darling, my treasure'. Phatik said softly, 'Mother, my holiday has come now I'm going home'.

For my next example I turn to his most famous short story, 'Kabuliwallah'. It touches what I believe to be the most sensitive of human relationships, that between father and daughter.

The Kabuliwallah, a dry fruit seller from Afghanistan, became friendly with a five-year-old Calcutta girl, Mini. In a fit of rage he stabbed a lying debtor and landed into jail. As the years rolled, he virtually faded from Mini's mind.

It was now her wedding day. The Kabuliwallah suddenly appeared and told her father that he had been let out of prison the previous evening and had brought for Mini a box of dry fruits. He begged to meet her, but the father declined. How could he entertain a murderer on an auspicious day ? The Kabuliwallah said, 'I brought this box of grapes and these nuts and raisins for the little one. Please give them to her.' When the father offered to pay for them he said:

> 'Please don't give me any money. Just as you have a daughter, so do I have one, in my own country. It is with her in mind that I came with a few raisins for your daughter : I didn't come to trade with you.'

Then he took from somewhere close to his heart a crumpled piece of paper. It was his daughter's handprint. The heart of Mini's father melted. He understood then that the rugged Afghan was a father just as he was a father and at once called for Mini.

The Kabuliwallah was utterly confused to see Mini in her bridal dress. But at last he smiled and said, 'Little one, are you going to your *svasur-bari* ?' Mini blushed and left the room.

"He suddenly understood clearly that his own daughter would have grown up too since the last he saw her, and with her too he would have to become re-acquainted."

"While the *sanai* went on playing inside the house, the Kabuliwallah sat in a Calcutta lane and pictured on to himself the barren mountains of Afghanistan."

I take for my last example another much anthologized short story of Tagore, 'Thakurda' or 'Grandfather'. It turns on the relationship between a grandfather and his parentless granddaughter who lived with him. The grandfather was Kailashchandra Roy Chaudhuri, a burnt-out descendant of the Babus of Nayanjor, who lived on the defunct glories of his ancestors. The granddaughter was Kusum who had no value in the marriage market on account of the penury of her grandfather. Thakurda was universally loved by his neighbours, but there was one man who despised him, the narrator of the story. He never considered Kusum worth him, but could not digest that Thakurda had not made the offering to him.

Out of malicious humour, he played a trick on the old man's vanity. He sent one of his friends dressed as the Lieutenant Governor to Thakurda, who sang praises of the Babus of Nayanjor to him. The old man easily fell to the guile and gave the last remaining treasures as parting gifts to the bogus Lieutenant Governor.

The narrator watched all this from the next room, and his ribs almost cracked with suppressed laughter. He ran into another room and hardly had collapsed into laughter when he saw Kusum choking with tears. She snapped, 'What has my grandfather done to you ? Why have you come to trick him ?' He now realised the revolting cruelty of his action. "He understood that in that house there was a girl with a human heart inside her, a heart whose array of feelings encompassed a land of mystery." And he was all the more touched when on the day following he heard her ask her grandfather, 'What did the Governor say to you yesterday ?' The old man cheerfully spun a long panegyric to the ancient house of the Nayanjor, supposedly delivered by the Lieutenant Governor. The girl received it eagerly.

When the narrator was alone with the grandfather he nervously and humbly made the proposal, "Although my own lineage was in no way comparable to the Babus of Nayanjor, yet...."

The old man clasped him to his breast and said joyfully, "I am poor—I never imagined I would have good fortune like this."

He wept as he spoke. This was the first time that he had forgotten his duty to his noble ancestors and admitted he was poor, admitted it would not do damage to the house of Nayanjor to accept him. The narrator had plotted to humiliate the old man, while he had longed for him, heart and soul, as the worthiest possible groom for his granddaughter.

The examples could be multiplied, but the such as I have given are enough to sustain my contention that Tagore's sensitivity to human pain is the greatest claim to his transcendental eminence as a short story writer and makes him level with the best in the world.

7

An Analysis of Intizar Husain's Short Story: 'Complete Knowledge' (*Poora Gyan*)

SHUBHA TIWARI

Intizar Husain's short story, 'Complete Knowledge' is a beautifully and effectively written short story in the tradition of 'Jatak Katha'. All Jataka tales narrate a moral tale through the experiences of a Bodhisattva, one destined to enlightenment. The tradition of 'Katha Vaachan' where a learned speaker tells a tale of knowledge and wisdom to attentive and eager listeners is based on stories of Hindu mythology. It is a pleasant surprise for the reader to find Intizar Husain using the tradition of Hindu mythological narrative telling in such an easy, effortless and simple manner. Trust and mutual regard between the narrator and listeners is the key to this tradition. The listeners believe in the superior knowledge of the narrator and accept it. The narrator knows the attitude of the listeners, and speaks purely out of the intention to benefit, inspire and train the listeners. As it is, nothing in traditional Indian culture and religion is ever practiced without any eye for utility. The vision is that of totality, merger, osmosis and synthesis. Everything, be they rituals, hymns, practices, ceremonies—everything comes packed with a purpose. The narrative of Intizar Husain in this story is cute for its simplicity. The wayward son of a Brahmin undergoes a headlong change of heart with just a few simple words of his father, 'Son, we are Brahmins. Knowledge is our wealth. Wisdom is our ornament a Brahmin must be a man of learning.'

His father's words pierced Manohar's heart like a spear. 'He renounced all his pleasures and bent over his books. He read the Vedas, the Puranas, the Ramanaya, and the Mahabharata; he read everything. In a short while he became a learned man' (22). How one wishes that life could be so simple where you say a few words to your son and he metamorphoses into a sincere boy! In this post-modern world of doubt and rebellion, and multiple layers of meanings, this Katha came to me as a gust of fresh wind. Here was a narrative that meant exactly what it said; I did not have to go on searching for unsaid messages as usually the post-modernist texts require that exercise.

The story is simply marvellous for many reasons. It begins with a loaded sentence, 'Manohar sat out on one path, but ended by taking an entirely different one' (22). How true it is for life! One hardly knows where one is going. You intend to do one thing but life presents something entirely different. Manohar is set on the path of knowledge by his father. Manohar feels that his knowledge is immense but the great indicator of unexplored knowledge comes from his father, 'And what about the things that haven't been written?' (22). Then follows a period of wandering for Manohar. A small but very significant paragraph symbolizes Manohar's quest but also the eternal human unfulfilment, the longing, the craving. Then comes another archetypal thirst quenching scene. A beautiful woman makes Manohar conscious of his thirst. Needless to say that this thirst is not only that of water. Manohar did not know that he was thirsty. It is the sight of the woman that makes him know his needs. But without fully realizing the meaning of this meeting, Manohar leaves her for acquiring knowledge. His soul remains restless as ever.

Manohar keeps roaming, searching, seeking, hungering for finding a meaning in life. This wandering, as myth critics tell us, has a deep embedded appeal for the collective psyche. Even the civilized man of today dreams of the nomadic wanderer going about caves, mountains, rocks and cliffs innovating, thinking and making life possible for himself. Manohar finally finds a Guru, whose name (as everything else in the story is very conventional and expected) is Sampoornanandji. His name means 'complete bliss'. Let us see as to what happens to his complete bliss.

Manohar asks the guru to give him peace of mind. The guru promptly tells him that peace blossoms from within and can be achieved only by meditation. For years together Manohar sits in meditation. But the thought of that voluptuous lady never leaves him. His meditation proves to be as futile as ever. At last, admitting defeat, he sits at the feet of his guru and begs him to give him *gyan* (enlightenment). Then follows a cycle of stories within the story. Guruji tries to improve Manohar by giving examples. Then come four stories of King Harcharan, Prajapati and Usha, Rishi Parashar and Vishvamitra and Menaka. All the four stories depict the woman as the cause of all evil in the world. The fall of man, his deviation from the path of duty and virtue are shown to have been caused by woman time and again. The woman is shown to have inexplicable power to change a man's mind. She can cause, what Italians call, thunderbolt. There is no remedy to the spell of fascination caused by a woman. If the man goes to the woman, he loses both the worlds. If he does not go to her, he remains unhappy and restless. It is a no win situation. Woman is presented as the opposite of all logic, reason and rationality. The stories bid Manohar not even talk to a woman. These highly suggestive and sensuous stories tell us about eroticism in the ancient Indian mind and literature. Pavan K. Varma and Sandhya Mulchandani write, 'Today, the philosophical acceptance of desire and the erotic sentiment has been asphyxiated by a hypocritical morality that has for much too long equated sex with sin and desire with guilt.' They say that we must have 'a glimpse of the sense of maturity and honesty that animated our ancestors.' And again. 'The absence of inhibition and guilt and the candour and boldness with which society set about seeking its pleasures find expression repeatedly in writings over the ages. The literature of India, both religious and secular, is full of sexual allusions, sexual symbolisms and passages of such frank eroticism the likes of which are not to be found elsewhere in world literature.' In this story also, limbs and gait of the woman are suggestively described. Each story ends with a tickling indication of union of man and woman and then the fall of man. The stories also create fear in the male mind regarding a woman and her contagious presence.

Manohar, however, fails to grasp anything and his yearning for the woman of his dreams increases day by day, moment by moment. The Guru gets fed up with the foolish boy and dismisses him. Manohar goes to the woman who had haunted him for years and unites with her. He blissfully lives with her. One day he recalls his father's words and returns to the guru for *gyan*. The guru, however himself was undergoing great mental turmoil regarding Manohar's behaviour and the fall of so many *sanyasis* (ascetics) because of the mysterious power of women. Sampoornanandji was agitated. When Manohar comes to him, he is startled by the serene, peaceful, gratified look of Manohar's beautiful face. Making Manohar sit at his place of worship, the Guru goes is search of a woman! The words of Sampoornanand that are refreshingly modern and flexible in approach are, 'Who has ever attained complete knowledge? Human beings must search for ever' (32). Human existence is always incomplete. Half-ness, craving, lacking, imperfection—these are human life. There is no need to force an unnatural roundness, and completion to anything related to human existence. There is no destination; the journey is the end. Defects are to be celebrated. The best that a human being can do is to keep on living, searching a meaning to life without losing hope and conviction. My pleasure in reading this story is that I did not expect such post-modernist message in a Jatak Katha.

This story written by Intizar Husain in 1960 and based on ancient Indian Jatak Kathas is so wonderfully open and trendy in its attitude. While the story goes on, the reader feels (especially if she is a woman) the depressing blames put on women. A woman simply exists. She does not do anything and yet she is held responsible for all misery and vices in the world. Needless to say that the ideas look bogus, off beat, rotten, unfair and dogmatic. They choke a woman as a sex object. Her very being, her body and breathing are held her crimes. But the end is to nice; it is simply superb. The mouth that poured venom on the woman at last craves for her. The creature that Sampoornanand cursed beckons him commandingly and he goes. However, the narrative attempts no hint at the will and wish of the woman concerned. The choice is all man's. The big question is whether a man should go to a woman or not; the thought that woman may also want to make her choices regarding her physical life and regarding her partner never occur to the writer; that a woman may also like to reject a relationship is nowhere in the mental makeup of the writer and it is quite natural. No one ever bothered about the likes and dislikes, whims and wishes, views and vows of a woman. There is no point in doing a feminist dissection of the piece.

On one hand, the end reinforces the fearful power of women, on the other hand, it tells us not to comment on things that we do not know. You have first to experience a thing in order to analyze it.

The traditional wisdom—Eastern, or Western—never fails to emphasize on the corrupting influence of women over guileless men. According to it, women compel men to deviate from the noble path. A woman is a distraction. Eve came under the influence of the infernal serpent, and forced innocent Adam to eat the forbidden apple and go against the divine will. Menaka ruined Vishvamitra's meditation, and thereby his future prospects of attaining godhood. The examples are numerous. Bhartrihari writes in *Shatakatrayam*,

> Discrimination's lucid light
> Continues to shine for learned men
> Only when it is not eclipsed
> By the tremulous lashes of women's eyes.

Similarly Rig Veda says, '...with women there can be no lasting friendship; their hearts are the hearts of jackals.' (Quoted by Varma and Mulchandani).

In the Indian context, the woman becomes either a 'devi' or a devil. The Indian mind rejects the middle path, where actually the truth lies. To me, the woman as the source of all evil, this dictum, underlies a deep-seated fear in the male psyche. The defencelessness, the helplessness, the utter futility of any effort, any protest before the charms of a woman, the realization of one's own weakness, and vulnerability has shaped the male mind to come to a conclusion that woman is the source of evil or rather woman is evil. The point to be noted, however, is that the cause of the fall (if deviation from the spiritual path be called a fall) lies with the male inadequacy to deal with a woman's raw appeal and not with the woman herself. Apart from this deep-rooted psychological fear, the narcissistic instincts of male dominated human existence refuse to recognize anything other than male. Female is held as the 'other' and the moment she is held as the 'other', all the hostility, reactionary approach, fear and what not crop up. I am reminded of the wonderful words of Gray Kochha-Lindgren, '...Narcissus longs only for the possession of the evanescent reflection of himself that shimmers in a glassy pond. This obsessive self-reflection leads not to the wisdom of self-understanding, which reflection so often claims for itself, but to death.... The narcissistic logic of this self-reflection, which is simultaneously murderous and suicidal, is a truncated symbolic dialectic that lacks the capacity to recognize that which is other than itself.'

Intizar Husain as a writer is an excellent example of his own kind. Away from the communal bitterness created by politicians out of selfishness, Husain was one of those who believed 'it was always possible for different communities to create a life of complex and pluralistic wholeness' (ix). He simply says, 'I am a Muslim, but I always feel that there is a Hindu sitting inside me' (xi). Accepting his heterogeneous Indian background, Husain says, 'I have no idea what a purely Islamic culture is' (x). Pained at the avoidable, unnecessary and tragic partition of our motherland, Husain never got used to a Lahore based, purely Pakistani existence. He compared fate-forced moving of his likes to Pakistan with *hijrat* (exodus) of the Prophet and his followers to Madina. Alok Bhalla, the translator of Husain's stories, in his brilliant analysis says, "He was not, he said, a man of strong religious beliefs, but the place where he had been born, the *basti* which had nurtured him in his childhood, still had its mysterious charm and pull. For him, *watan* (homeland). He insisted, was not merely defined by the territory within which he now claimed his rightful citizenship, it was also the larger civilizational space from which he derived his imaginative strength. That is why, he said sadly, as if echoing the sentiments of countless migrants during the partition, 'I still feel that I am an exile who wanders between Karbala and Ayodhya.' " I should add that his Ayodhya was not a real place on some political map, but the utopian kingdom of Rama, 'where an examined life of truth and moral law alone can confirm god's presence; and his Karbala was not the present city with a specific geographical location, but a richly imagined site where the traditions of the Prophet gave life a coherence, a reason and a balance' (xii).

The stories of Husain and this story in particular underline a fundamental principal of life that the most difficult thing in this life is to be easy, simple and good. The ordinary things are not all that ordinary. Life is all about making mistakes, learning from those mistakes, being kind to others, not to burn in revenge and hatred all the time, and enjoy doing common things. Religion, philosophy, rituals, nationhood, identity—all these concepts are valid only when they spread love, peace, and make life livable. If religion, and ideology break the social fabric and mental peace of individuals, they are useless.

The very title of the story 'Poora Gyan' point the flexible approach of Husain. Instead of Sanskrit word, 'gyan' he could have used the Urdu work 'ilm' in order to establish himself as a *pucca* Urdu writer. But he does not do so. So it goes with the sources of his stories. I wish to quote Bhalla at length, 'Trying to give shape to his unique understanding of the Muslim identity in the Indian subcontinent, Intizar Husain draws freely and imaginatively upon the rich and fascinating narrative traditions of the Indian subcontinent found in such diverse sources as the Kathasaritsagar, Puranic lore, Sufi legends, religious epics, Jataka tales, popular lore about talking animals and birds, Hatamtai, anecdotes about rishis, who have the learning to challenge the gods but are yet fallible.' A thoroughly modern writer, he uses them to reflect upon religious faith and identity, historical truths and modern delusions, power and the endless failure of reason. Thus, in his telling of the Jatakas, he points out how difficult it is in the present to locate the 'good' and on the basis of our understanding of it, perform the right action in the public realm. In the older Jatakas both these actions are unproblematic. The good is unambiguously located in the Bodhisattva and is available to in every generation to all living things. The Bodhisattva is reborn as a man, a woman, a king, a woodcutter, a witch, a tree or a monkey. Each reincarnation of the Bodhisattva reasserts the fact that good is eternally available and each story about him recalls for us the fact, which we tend to forget, that ordinary people, with the most limited of intellectual and material resources, can always recognize the good man and follow his example. The Bodhisattva of these tales is the ideal man whose personal inwardness is never distinct from his public actions. He is a self-governing moral agent who always acts responsibly towards the rest of creation.

In Intizar Husain's rendering of the Jatakas, one is at first enchanted by the tranquility of the forest and by the silence of the bhikshus who walk through them. Unlike the listeners of the old Jatakas, we are located in world which is noisy and agitated. Intizar Husain startles us by reminding us of the fact that even though we live in cities, the realm of trees, birds, rivers, animals, and the sky is in our neighbourhood and that we are both dependent on it and responsible for it.... In the old Jatakas, such a lesson would have been enough to make people see, in the world around them, signs of the divine presence. The pilgrims of Intizar Husain, however are like us....

The bhikshus in Intizar Husain's stories understand the lessons taught to them, but they do not know how to act correctly. They fail to understand that an action is 'right' only if it is based in the 'good'. A good man can, at times, make mistakes without jeopardizing his goodness, but a man who has not achieved wisdom can perform the right action and yet bring disaster upon himself and others. The bhikshus in Jatakas, who found themselves in the presence of the Bodhisattva, never went back to their old ways of ignorant living. The bhikshus in Intizar Husain's stories are told a countless number of moral tales, but fail to recognize how the 'good' can be achieved in the world in which they live. They cannot reconcile the beauty of the world and the joy of the senses with the demands of renunciation; the demands of humanity with the fear of entrapment in the vast network of illusions. Like many of the protagonists in his Partition tales, they find themselves staring at blank spaces where identities are utterly confused. At the end they give up their quest and are stranded on the border between forests and villages, rational knowledge and uncontrolled passion, religious faith and despair. The learned man of 'Complete Knowledge' thinks that evil will always be with us and is paralyzed by that knowledge... (xvii).

Sampoornanand has no answer to raw sexuality. His 'gyan' proves inadequate in dealing with the demands of the body. But the funniest part is that sexuality has been bracketed with evil. My argument is against this foolish presumption. The whole Indian psyche is pervaded by concepts of evil, sin, guilt and fall when it comes to man-woman relationship. The healthy spirit of sharing, understanding, intimacy, caring and reciprocity is totally missing. Man-woman relationship is weighed in terms of domination, exploitation, power, money, winning and losing. Emotions have been thrown out of the window. Relationships are bound to prove inadequate and unsatisfying in such a scenario. Although much has changed; still unfortunately basic Indian mentality remains the same.

WORKS CITED

Gray Kochhar-Lindgren. 1993. *Narcissus Transformed—The Textual Subject in Psychoanalysis and Literature.* Pennsylvania: The Pennsylvania State University Press.

Intizar Husain. 2002. *A Chronicle of Peacocks—Stories of Partition, Exile and Lost Memories.* New Delhi: Oxford University Press.

Pavan Varma and Sandhya Mulchandani. 2004. *Love and Lust—An Anthology of Erotic Literature from Ancient and Medieval India.* New Delhi: Harper Collins, *India Today.*

8

MAN-WOMAN RELATIONSHIP IN *GODAN*

SADHANA AGRAWAL

Godan, a last masterpiece of peasant India, is undoubtedly one of the most outstanding novels of Premchand in *Godan.* Premchand presents "the true and vivid picture of India". It is Premchand who developed a new trend in Hindi fiction to write sincerely about social realities, particularly the realities concerning the lives of the vast peasant masses of this country. In *Godan,* Premchand not only painted a pathetic picture of the plight of hungry and semi-starved Indian peasantry but also exposed a scene of sarcastic and ironical conversations with man-woman.

The novel *Godan* has its own peculiarities to enthrall the reader and one may easily go deep into the depth of it to find out precious pearls. The attraction lies in the novel not for its vividness but for its unbroken sequence of events. This will give us immense pleasure of a filmy scenario if our fancy is a little more alive to catch a glance of the scene *Godan* was depicted with a deep understanding, the tragic life of the peasants on one side and the oppressive laws of the *Zamindar* at the other. The life of the poor and oppressed is "due to keeping on good terms with the master that the trouble has remained at arm's length from us" (5). The safest way is "to keep on tickling his feet" (5). In addition to these Premchand unraveled the secret philosophy of love, the man-woman relationship was not also untouched and it requires a deep and serious study.

The present paper endeavours to unfold the man-woman relationship in *Godan* by sketching the characters either in love or married. Premchand remarked at one place that the novel is only a portrait of human character, hence "to throw light on human character and to unfold his secrets are the basic essence of the novel" (Guru: 107) and the writing "is an effort to discover, to underline and convey the true significance of things". Man-woman relationship being the central subject of literature appears to be inexhaustible and the changing times and changing social situations have served to bring out its amazing diversity and infinity variety. A number of pairs have been portrayed exposing man-woman relationship to love and marriage. Among them some are—Hori and Dhania, Gobar and Jhunia, Matadin and Selia, Bhola and Nohri, Sona and Mathura, Rupa and Ramsevak, Khanna and Govindi, Mehta and Malti.

Hori-Dhania, Sona-Mathura and Rupa-Ramsevak are married couples in social milieu of village. Hori and Dhania lead their life enduring equally their rare smiles and unceasing sorrows and their frustrations and hopes. They have differences ever now and then, show their resentment, and talk jovially also. As Dhania said shyly, "What a dashing youth you are to think that young girls should fall for you!" (6). Hori replied, "Do you think I have grown old? I am not forty yet. Men are not men before sixty" (6) and soon the flippancy of Hori vanished and says sadly, "Dhania, I shall never get to the age of sixty" (6). Soon Dhania became restless listening such words and said reproachfully, "Don't utter such ominous words. Even if I say something good, I only get hard words in return" (6-7).

"Hori's dispirited remarks had shaken her wounded heart to the very core" (7). In point of fact the cruel words of Hori are very true but Premchand interrogated: "Can a two-eyed ever feel the hurt that a one-eyed man feel at the taunt of being called a one-eyed man?" (7). Facing and enduring all critical situations in their life, Hori and Dhania never lose their balance. They struggle hard to face the realities as their fate destines. But one strong and persistent desire to have a cow is not fulfilled in spite of struggling hard. The last scene where Hori is on his death bed becomes more pathetic and moves the sensitive hearts when his devoted and truthful wife, Dhania realizes the fading shadows of hope, soon rises like a machine to bring out twenty annas that she has, places the coins in the icy palm of her husband for fulfilling his last wish of *Godan*, looks at Datadin and says (352) and collapses to the ground, not in a moment the pathetic feelings of the hearts burst out into tears.

At the first encounter Gobar and Jhunia establish their love claims to each other. Chapter V unfolds their amorous talking and Premchand's views on "selfless love, for which he could live and die; love not fitful like a glowworm's but slow and steady like the flame of an earthen lamp" (43). Witty Jhunia asks Gobar, "To get all he has to give all" (43). Further she warns, "You'll have to be mine. And then if I see you begging before others I'll give you up for ever,"(43) and

> To pass my days with one man is the one pleasure of my life. It's men who spoil their wives. If a husband runs after women it's natural for his wife to exchange glances with other men.... Can you keep a wife under lock and key and play the fool of yourself? What you do openly she'll do secretly? (47)

Jhunia's talk opens windows on a world entirely new to Gobar. Gobar is ready to suffer even ostracism for such a sensible girl like Jhunia. "It was a big wide world and if they threw him out he could live in another village" (43). Gobar and Jhunia decides "to be steadfast in love" (44).

This amorous love of them remains steadfast from their early insane stage to the path of duty until Gobar in city understands "Jhunia was his only diversion" (271). She is fed up with this sort of life "She had no one to talk to except Gobar who, selfishly enough, still made physical demands on her" (271). She needs solitude, she suffers from frequent headaches. She loses appetite. She has not even the strength to push her child from her breast. Her child, Lallu dies of diarrhoea. The memory of Lallu tortured her and "while alive, Lallu was a burden to her, but after death he had become a part of her life" (272). This ruins their heavenly pleasures as Gobar remains unsatisfied and Jhunia "had completely withdrawn into herself; outwardly, no more than an automation" (272). With this regard Premchand says:

> By sharing her grief, by probing into her afflicted heart, Gobar could have come closer to her. But he stopped short

at the barren shores of her outward life, not caring to enter the great sea of her heart and he went away thirsty. (272)

In consequence of it Gobar starts to take up drinking, returns home late at night, abuses Jhunia on any crazy pretext, and sometimes beats her.

"Jhunia", Premchand says, "had begun to suspect that Gobar did not regard her any better-than a keep.... What a sad blunder to have eloped with him; the whole world had laughed at her, and she gained nothing by it" (273). Gobar became "utterly selfish and heartless and she meant nothing more to him than an object for his physical gratification" (277). Living together "they were a hundred miles apart. A wide gulf yawned between the two. They made it a point to misunderstand each other. They nursed petty grudges" (277).

Premchand remarks pathetically: "Gobar had treated her like a tyrant, abused and beat her; but when she saw him, her heart melted. He lay like a cripple, helpless, she bent over the bed and gazed at him with sad eyes" (279). Hearing Gobar's grazing Jhunia wails "What have they done to my husband!" (279). At the very moment seeing Jhunia standing before him Gobar requests her, "Forgive me, God has punished me, I treated you badly" (28). She takes care of her husband, earns bread and despite such day long hard work remains happy. "A gush of joy overtook her within a month she felt transformed; gone was her lethargy; her limbs once again became supple; and a glow on her cheeks" (281).

With the help of Gobar-Jhunia relationship, Premchand unravels that Gobar "has been cruel to a near and dear one, a new life stirs his soul and he is restless to atone for his sin" (281). He decides to change his own nature to be kind and humble and "realized that the opportunity to be of service to others came one's way with rare good fortune and he had every mind to take advantage of such an opportunity to the fullest" (281).

The relationship of Matadin and Selia is based on love. Matadin is Brahmin and Selia Cobbler. Due to caste differences no one in village accepts their relationship. However, Mahabharata and the Puranas have examples of "Brahmins who had married girls of lower castes, and proved that children were accepted as Brahmins" (242). Though unmarried, in the eyes of world Selia belongs to Matadin. Depressed, deserted and desolated Selia endures all cruelties of her family patiently and even Matadin's blow not to "cast a glance at her evil face" (248) and decides not to "give up the Pandit. Let him starve me, beat me, kill me. I can't leave him. I prefer death to becoming someone else's woman" (247). It is her true love and belief that one day Matadin repents and strikes that "he was being punished for being cruel to Selia" (292) and comes back to her hut and says: "This is our house; this is my temple" (335) and keeps promise not to go away after making the votive offering of a *'lotaful'* of water. "As long as I am alive I shall live with you, and worship you" (335). At last he exposes himself out of benevolence, "All those who fulfil their *'dharma'* are Brahmins, all those who violate their *'dharma'* are cobblers" (336).

On a sun-shiny, crystal, clear, conjugal life of Mrs. & Mr. Khanna, Malti shadows over them just like a patch of dark cloud, Premchand remarks:

> The relations between Khanna and his wife Govindi were always strained. Why the relations were strained, is not so easy to say. Astrologers said there was a conflict in their stars, although before their marriage the pundits had taken every care to see that their horoscopes tallied perfectly. According to the science of love, there could be some other reason for the differences between husband and wife, and the psychologists world possibly have given their own version. But the fact remained that their relations were strained. (182)

But Premchand knows rather better of them for being so strained. He knows that Govindi is not a slave of luxuries, keeps herself occupied in "bringing up the children and looking after the household" and "so engrossed was she in these that her mind never wandered to luxurious concoctions. He was not a toy: she had no desire to make herself look voluptuous. If her husband did not have the sense to see her intrinsic beauty and ran after gay 'society' girls, that was his misfortune" (182). The wall of wealth, rising higher daily, is the main problem that threatens their conjugal life. Premchand himself condemns

Mr. Khanna, as "Polite and beaming with his clients, Khanna was systematically rude and inflammable at home. Politeness to him was no more than an appendage, a weapon to cheat the world with; it was not something ingrained in his character" (182-83). Often he speaks rudely to Govindi and when she finds his rudeness unbearable, retires to her room and passes the night weeping. In spite of all this Khanna is everything to her and she cannot think of life without him.

Feeling insulted Govindi decides not to stay in a house "where she had to put up with persistent ill treatment" (185) and "where insults are heaped on me" (191). She relates her woe to Mehta: "Life has become intolerable for me. I have put up with suffering till now. I can bear it no more. Malti is bent on ruining me. I've no weapon to fight her with.... Today I left home, determined never to return.... I have kept my anguish in my heart. Today, I beg you, I beg you with folded hands, save me from Malti" (189-90). Mehta convinces her that he will do anything for her and urges her to return home: "No, Deviji. That's your home and will always remain your home. You have created it, you have given life to it. Motherhood enjoys the most exalted status in life. In such an exalted position, one is above insult or humiliation. A mother gives life. What does it matter to her whether somebody is annoyed with her or shouts at her?" (191-92).

Much more devoted than before, Govindi keeps herself occupied in household and it is only her love and sacrifice that wins at last. Betrayed and derailed Mr. Khanna comes to his senses only when his mill has burnt down. His deeply wounded heart finds solace hearing Govindi's words: "Why are you disheartened? Money is the root of every evil, the destroyer of the soul. After all what did we gain by being rich? While you were rich you had not even the time to talk to your children or write letter to relatives. A true man does not bow his head before wealth. He loves truthfulness, justice, sacrifice, and perseverance. If these qualities were missing in a man, the world would think him a cheat and shut its doors on him" (287-88). She adds further, "I'm happy this load is off your chest. Real happiness lies in making others happy. To my mind, it is always better to be the oppressed than to be the tyrant. Till now your object in life has been to further your own interests. Please don't misunderstand me" (288). Govindi is thankful to God that He has opened the door leading him to a pure and ideal life depriving him of such wealth.

Mehta and Malti, the heart of *Godan* appear first time in chapter VI on the occasion of festival celebrated in Rai Saheb's house. A strange vividness lies in both. Mehta, looks "every inch of a philosopher" (53), as says Malti, is known for his own intellectuality and frankness while Malti is known as butterfly. Premchand calls her "vivacious, lavishly made up, witty, forward, well up in the ways of men, fond of the good things of life, coquettish—in short very modern" (53). A similarity is found between Mehta and Malti in the beginning. Both consider life a play. Mehta says:

> I look at life as a magnificent sport, where there is not place for censure, jealousy and bitterness. I don't brood over the past, I don't worry about the future. The present is the only thing, which has any meaning for me.... Where there is life, activity, joy and love, there is God. To make life happy is the true worship and right deliverance.... The knowledge which kills the soul is not knowledge but a grinding stone. (191)

And Premchand writes about Malti in chapter XV:

> To all appearances a "butterfly" Malti was in fact bee-frugal and diligent. Her life was not just a round of gaiety; one doesn't live all the time on sweets. For her, fun was not the penultimate of life, nor self-interestedness. But frivolity certainly helped to soften life's oppressiveness. (146)

Joviality is an ultimate goal for Mehta and a means for Malti. Mehta considers free love just a thing for the development of the mind and marriage "a sacramental contract"—He says further, "Man has no right to break it, nor woman. You are a free agent before you enter the contract. Once you are in it, that's that"? (58). Chance brings Mehta and Malti very close. Accompanying with Malti to *shikar,* Mehta focuses on the modern ways of woman: "Modern girls don't need men's protection. They walk hand in hand with them" (69). In jungle they walk and talk happily and express their views. Mehta asks Malti, "Am I so wicked? And if I say I love you, will you marry me?"(71). Looking him tenderly Malti says, "But how could I marry a log of wood? You'd nag your wife all day" (71). At this Mehta agrees, and replies, "You are right, Malti I am not much of a success with women. If a woman is false, I can see through her, and then I lose interest in her" (71). About Malti, he is of the view, "You are intelligent, clever, kind, witty and vivacious. You can do everything but love" (71).

Pure and simple life of the countryside always fascinates Mehta. Even in the jungle seeing a young *'jungli'* woman he does not hesitate to applaud her qualities and shows his reverence:

> I've great respect for this girl. Pull out my eyes if I look at her lustfully. Even for my most intimate friends I wouldn't have climbed so high in the heat. And she has done all this for a chance visitor. She would have taken this trouble even for a poor woman. I write and speak volumes on universal brotherhood and universal love. But she practices it. Professing is so much easier than practicing it. (75)

It seems it is not youth and health and seductive charms but love, devotion and sacrifice of a *real* woman that attract Mehta and he gets surprised to see Malti's rude behavior towards this young girl.

In Chapter XIII, Mehta admits, "A woman's sympathy can change defeat into victory" (134). And "Miss Malti is pretty, gay, intelligent, broad-minded and many other things besides. But the qualities I seek in my life's partner are missing in her. In my idea, a wife should be an embodiment of sincerity and self-abnegation who effaces her own individuality and merges herself with her husband's personality; the body is of the husband and the soul that of the wife" (135). With this regard Premchand opines:

> If a man richly takes on the qualities of a woman he becomes a Mahatma. But if a woman imbibes the qualities of a man she becomes evil. A man is really attracted only towards a woman who possesses the essential attributes of a woman. (135)

Through the characters of Mehta and Malti Premchand wants to depict the real picture of relations what man expects from woman: "Even if I kill her there should be no spirit of retaliation or violence in her. Even if I love another woman in her presence it should not rouse her jealousy (135-36). In all conditions woman should remain faithful and steadfast to man. One day he will realize her true worth and worship her for it. Mehta remarks, "I don't want a wife who can discuss Einstein or proof-read my books. I want a wife to elevate my soul and make my life pure" (136). He considers Mrs. Khanna a truthful woman. But Mrs Khanna says:

> Forget that woman is superior to man. Man is superior to woman. He who bears the burden of the family. He stirs the spirit of service and sacrifice in woman. If he lacked these qualities, a woman would not have them either. The spirit of revolt that you find in woman today is taking roots because man himself has lost these qualities. (157)

Premchand here condemns both man and woman for wanting high spirits that they need. Mehta suggests:

> True joy and real consolation proceed from selfless service. Selfless service is the fountainhead of rights; the source of power. Service is that cement which keeps a married couple locked in love and common ideals. Where service is lacking you have distrust. (155)

Khanna's attraction towards Malti is only a delusion. He says sadly to Rai Saheb, "It's vain to hope that she knows what love is" (229). Further he adds, "I've ruined my home for her sake, *Bhai Saheb*. It's years that I've talked to Govindi intimately. I've developed the same apathy towards her that long-suffering patient develops for sweets.... But even then I hovered like a moth around the flame of her beauty" (230). Malti herself says to Mr. Khanna plainly: "Remember one thing: no man ever won a woman's love with the help of money." (236)

A change has come over Malti living in contact with Mehta. Mehta also feels the same change. Both come to the conclusion that the golden path of service is the only practical principle, which can give meaning to life. Malti realizes, "Till Mehta came into her life all the men with whom Malti came into contact had only excited her sensual side. Under his influence, her dormant spirit of self-sacrifice and helpfulness surfaced" (298). Malti is no longer a *butter-fly* and "She would often visit poor patients without charging fees; besides, her behaviour towards them mellowed" (298). Simple village life also leaves an ever lasting imprint on her mind. She feels a new living spirit among the villagers. She remarks, "They worked the whole day, went without food, and yet they put up a cheerful front. With their love, they had made others their own and effaced themselves for the sake of others. They lived for their children, their husbands, their relatives" (300).

Mehta attracts towards Malti seeing her new face. Undoubtedly she has in a way dedicated herself to him. "But the more he saw of Malti, the more he felt pulled towards her. He knew that he did not lay much store by beauty, that only virtue had any meaning for him" (301). Seeing Malti in the midst of the village women for the first time he experiences a feeling of inexplicable oneness with her. Holding her hand in his, he says that she comes into his thoughts, not once, but again and again—"like fragrance floating on wind, like imagination in flight" (303). But as she remarks: "You have looked at me with the eyes of a cynic; never with the eyes of a lover. Don't you know even this much that a woman wants to be loved, not tested? A critic finds faults even in virtues and makes a beautiful thing look ugly. A lover can see virtue in vice and beauty in ugliness. I loved you: it never occurred to me that you could never be weak. But you thought me shifty, frivolous, mean, despicable. You kept a safe distance from me. No, listen to me. Why am I frivolous? And shifty? Because I didn't get that sort of love which could make me steadfast and serious. If only you had loved me the way I loved you!" (303). Mehta opens his heart before her and says, "The deeper I've gone, and the larger the pearls I've found. I came to you to while away my time, but I stayed as a worshipper" (304). Malti gives more importance to love and looking into his eyes says, "I think true love is always above suspicion—for suspicion always leads to violence. Love demands complete surrender. In the temple of love rewards go to the devotee, not the critic" (305).

Mehta has found a chance to analyze himself after this blow. During this period Malti has felt self-satisfaction in devotion and Mehta voluptuousness. Malti keeps herself occupied in household and Mehta watches her wistfully not in the form of a woman but in the form of a mother also. He is amazed to see her tender affection towards a sick child, Mangal. Malti shows her great respect for Mehta and says passionately, "Before you came into my life, pleasures lured me. You taught me there were deeper things, nobler things. You gave me a richer meaning to my life. I'm grateful to you for all this.... I could cherish nothing more in the world than your love and trust, they mean my life's fulfilment" (328).

"How full of solace and magic they were?" (328). Mehta has experienced by his heart as her words fell into his ears. She begins to regard ephemeral pleasures as life's supreme truths. She finds a new vision of life in service. Premchand's words all of a sudden burst out and Mehta starts praising her: "No, not of stone, but a living goddess—of sacrifice, of many mercies" (329). She is of the opinion that she has done this sacrifice out of her own interest as it elevates her heart and perhaps it satisfies her vanity.

Malti's expressions become grave when at last she says "that we shall be far happier as friends. I know you love me, trust me, would sacrifice your life for me.... For your sake no sacrifice is too big for me. Let us pray to God that He keeps us steadfast in our love. By setting up a home of our own, by confining our souls in a cage, by living for ourselves alone, how can we ever hope to reach what both of us wish ready to reach—the infinite?" (330).

She doesn't tell that conjugal love is worthless but attachment leads to desire, desire to selfishness. She says that if they get enmeshed in desires, their sphere of humanity will certainly shrink the day. She earnestly prays to Mehta: "Your learning, your love of humanity will lead the way; I'll follow. I beg you to do this. If your mind goes towards worldliness, I'll try to persuade you away from it; if I fail, I shall at least know the greatness of my failure.... But of one thing I am sure: I will no longer be a prey to worldly desires" (330).

Mehta agrees with Malti and realizes reality of life. Feeling as one, their hearts embrace and merge and forget their identity for a moment and soon their grave minds determine to remain single for life long, get separated in the interest of society.

Premchand has no match in representing the most realistic interpretation of the man-woman relationships on the plain surface. He pours out his vigorous heart and mind over his alive and sensitive characters. *Godan* is thus the outcome of Premchand's mature thinking and deep feeling in which his consciousness for the welfare of human being sours high. The woman in *Godan* is conscious of *'Self'*. The devoted hardworking peasants demand their rights in *Godan*. The embodiment of love, sacrifice and dutiful woman demands love. The dutiful souls demand happiness and peace for all.

REFERENCES

1. Prem Chand. 2002. *Godan.* Trans. Jai Ratan and P. Lal. Mumbai: Jaico Publishing House.
2. Rajeshwar Guru. 1976. *Godan.* New Delhi: Radhakrishna Prakashan.

9

WOMAN IN *DEODAS*

RANJANA CHANANA

In this paper, an attempt is made to study Saratchandra Chatopadhyaya's women protagonists portrayed in 'Deodas' with a view to understand and appreciate their trails and tribulations, heart and soul, intelligence and knowledge under the impact of the conflicting influence of tradition and awakening modernity and to critically analyze their response to the emerging situation in life so as to find a room in the contemporary society. Parbati and Chandramukhi are the chief center of attraction in the novel. The novel opens on a scorching afternoon with Devdas, the Zamindar's son and Parbati, a neighbour's daughter who often gives company to Devdas who has been denied the freedom to join friends for once he goes out he seldom returns. He plays truant. An affectionate bond grows between them as they pass most of their time together. Devdas is sent to Calcutta for studies. After years he comes back as a handsome young man with a fashionable life style. Parbati's grandmother fancies a marriage between these two childhood friends but the proposal is rejected outright on the ground of differences on social status. Parbati's marriage is fixed elsewhere with a elderly widower, Bhubanmohan Choudhary, whose children are of her age. Desperate and disappointed but full of hope and confidence that 'her Deva' will not let her go to any other man, she takes a bold step to step in his room at midnight to reveal her sincere love to him without caring for the family slander and scandal in the society. Dev is amazed to see her in his room at odd hours and tries to crush her fiery spirit by his piercing words:

> "Don't you feel shame in coming along here midnight?" (*Deodas*; Translated 29)

Parbati firmly tells him:

> "Not at all, why should I feel shame?"(29)

Their mutual conversation comes to an end with Devdas's inability to face up to parental opposition and with a promise to talk to his father over the matter the next day. In the morning, getting a very rude response from his father, he goes away to Calcutta.

Parbati on receiving the news gets a strong blow in her heart. She finds herself utterly dejected and deserted. Saratchandra probes into feminine psyche through the character of Parbati. Parbati is aware of the injustice done to her by Deva who proves to be an anti-hero in the crisis of life. She is alienated but her self-conceit never allows her emotions and feelings to lurk outside, as she can never become an object of pity. She suffers internally but in spite of surrounded by sea of troubles she still has a ray of hope that Dev will come back and accept her by rejecting the parental opposition. But to her surprise, her hope does not linger for long. After two days of departure Dev writes a letter to Parbati regretting his inability to marry her. He also writes that he never had a great love for her and that he never liked her and had never thought of marrying her. He does not feel sorrow in his heart after coming away from her. She should better try to forget him and God will help her in getting success.

Parbati tries to conceal her feelings of dejection and keeps mum. The inner conflict goes on. The novel explores and deals with the psychic turmoil of her within the limiting and restricting domesticity. She is no doubt a bold lady but now has become the victim of series of incidents. Her revolutioned soul would have revolted against Zamindar's social status and she would have been victorious if Devdas cooperates. She is essentially lonely and sensitive. The isolation and insecurity that she suffers is human. She is a firm determined lady. The psychic travails of the strange and cheated self indicates a measured and specified movement from self-desertion to self-assertion. Now she has made up her mind to become Mrs. Choudhary. Devdas after posting the letter finds him to be in a different frame of mind. He realises his love for Parbati—Paro—the nickname given to her out of love. He rushes to the village, meets her at the ghat, apologizes and expresses his desire to marry. But is a different Paro that he sees. She blurts out:

> I have no faith in you. The man I am going to—he is wealthy, wise calm and patient. He is a religious man. My parents want the best for me; so they would never have me fall into the hands of someone as ruthless, reckless and unwise as you. Now please let me go. (41)

Thus she rejects him in a haughty way and departs.

Parbati's firm decision and arrogance and Devdas's indecision invite unmitigated suffering for both. Parbati is welcomed in a big mansion as the wife of an elderly widower Bhubanmohan Choudhary and his grown up children. She stands at the cross roads of time. She becomes the mother of three children of her own age within the few moments of her entrance into her husband's home. She seeks change within the cultural norms, seeks not to interpret them but merely to make them alive with dignity and self-respect. She seeks anchorage in marriage. She perceives it as an alternative to the bondage imposed by the parental family and opts for it. Soon thereafter he realizes that another replaces one restrictive set up. She is caught in the conflict between responsibility to oneself and conformity to the traditional role of a wife. She does not accept to be considered merely as the object of gratification or worship. There is ample evidence in the text indicating her leading a sexless but life full of adoration and reverence. She has forgotten her moments of obstinacy and arrogance. She becomes the object of pity for her husband who tenderly taking her face in his hands, gazes into it for a long time utters these words with a sigh on the lips:

> 'Oh, no, I didn't do the right thing.'
>
> 'Which thing?'
>
> 'I was just thinking—with your beauty and youth, you have not come to the right place.' (55)

Saratchandra's rare insight into the character reveals the secret of untold story of struggle of a young woman who instead of getting love and marital bonds seeks the blessings of her husband just like a little daughter with the belief in conformity and compromise for the sake of the retention of domestic harmony rather than revolt which might result in the disruption of family relationship. Paro generally tries to come out of frustration and disappointments along with the traditional concept that the sole purpose of a wife existence is to please her husband heartily (if not physically). It reveals her capacity to assert own rights and individuality and become fully aware of her potential as a human being. The novelist is successful in presenting the transformation which creeps in her life to show how she finds a way out, awakens, comes alive, moves into future to lead a new life—the life of a responsible wife and mother. She achieves a sense of profound freedom and fulfilment through the realization of her autonomy in the premises of her big home. She tries to satisfy her elder married daughter and wins her heart by her nobility and sound behaviour, which they never expected, from a step-mother. Bhubanmohan Choudhary worships her as a Goddess and blesses her for saving him from self-reproach. Thus she leads her life with her sense of certainty, confidence and assurance.

One day she learns about the sad demise of Jamindar Narayan Mukharjee—the father of Devdas and reaches her mother's home. She gets a chance to see Deva and meet him in order to pacify him and his mother but she was shocked to hear about Deva's life in Calcutta, which proves to be a living hell for him. Deva's addiction for the world of alcohol and his liking for the courtesan breaks her heart again in small fragment. Instead of pacifying Deva, she starts disdaining him. After a short while she starts repudiating herself a thousand times. She accuses herself for all this. Her repentance and inner struggle increases by leaps and bounds. She felt her life has no meaning, no honour for taking the responsibility of the homes of others while her own life—her Deva—is being destroyed but for the help and support of anybody in his life. She is playing the role of a patron and benefactor and one who is her own is starving. She decides to die at the feet of Deva by breaking her forehead. She is not now an arrogant personality. Saratchandra's awareness with woman psychology reveals many layers of ups and downs, acceptance and rejection, failure and success, beyond measure in the life of a woman. Her dropping tears cannot give the account of commotion, tumult, anarchy, tempest, perplexity, agitation, and turmoil inside her soul. The agony of her soul breaks her lips that she is a housewife or a stone, she knows better about herself. She tries her best to restore the paralyzed life of Dev by advising him to marry a girl. She advises him not to drink. The struggle is continuously going on in her heart. She cannot resist her from asking Deva for spending profuse money in buying ornaments for a woman. Deva's comment on Paro for not wearing any ornament and her destitute response takes the reader into the dark, cloudy, unshiny, helpless, dependent heart of Paro.

Deva's interaction focuses on the various issues. We find Parbati as the embodiment of true lover and traditional woman who try to conceal her love and expresses her sympathy in an uncontrollable manner. Parbati considers Deva a paragon among men despite all his faults as he is considered to be ineffectual, weak willed, always in a perpetually melancholic state. Devdas puts a proposal of running away tonight with Parbati who denies after pondering over the matter. It is not possible for Paro, who is the symbol of ideal wife. Here lies the Indian sensibility in woman who may suffer and suffer alone but will not allow a blot on character or family only for her love, her interest. Deva leaves Parbati after promising to meet her once before his death.

Chandramukhi—the so-called prostitute—the bad woman, the destroyer of man, the solace of the frustrated in love is in no way less important than Parbati—the chief protagonist in the novel. Deva goes to the prostitute in order to get peace of heart, as he feels restless for a long time since Parbati is married to someone else. Chandramukhi is considered to be the most beautiful and rich prostitute in the whole area of Chitpur. On meeting Chandramukhi for the first time, Dev comments:

> Chunnibabu, in which hell you have brought me! (5)

Chandramukhi and Chunnibabu are speechless. Casting a glance full of hatred at Chandramukhi Dev utters:

> "Hush! How uncivilized, how ugly, deformed she looks? (5)

Chandramukhi is stunned for a moment. She is not an ordinary prostitute and she is eloquent in speech. None dares to insult her in such manner. She never allows an opportunity to anybody to commit such sin before her. But today she becomes stupid and unintelligent. She has been meeting thousands of people of different nature since last ten years but she has never met such a fantastic, curious odd individual full of idiosyncrasies. He gives her a hundred-rupee note and hurriedly went away down the stairs. Chandramukhi, since the very moment is attracted towards Devdas. She finds him infinitely charming. She says of his company that there is not a woman on earth who would deny herself this heaven. She requests Chunnibabu to bring his friend here again and accepts that she is really in love with this strange fellow.

On her second meeting with Devdas, Chandramukhi requests him not to drink too much wine as the strong intoxication spoils the life. With the advancement of time, she realizes that Dev is a deserted lover. Dev draws her sympathy and talking about woman and her greatness enters into deep slumber. The moment changes the life of the prostitute. The woman in her awakens, she realizes that she has attached and involved herself in multiple ways to Devdas like any other human being. She feels that till now she has been busy in the business of love-making but today she loves someone sincerely. She sells the belongings of her rich house along with all the ornaments, which she now does not require. Devdas's attention is drawn towards a wonderful and astonishing change in the atmosphere of the house—without chair, mirror, wardrobe and objects of decorations. It is appearing to be a lifeless house. He is unable to tolerate the adversity and sorry plight. For Chandramukhi it is 'her fortune'. The adverse condition is the result of a pre-planned life of the prostitute. Can a woman of bad name and fame may change so soon and why? These are the questions, which take us to peep into the woman psychology. Life of Chandramukhi is changed after a brief meeting of five minutes with Devdas. His indomitable spirit and courage to bear the frustrated love of Parbati has touched her soul near the surface and she decides to serve him if fortune helps her and opportune her. She neither shares her views with anybody nor takes long time to decide her fate. Like a sincere lover she waits to meet Devdas for the last time before leaving the place and god has granted her prayers. She has the deep trust that Devdas will surely come once. Devdas never imagines that a prostitute will change the way of her life for him and wait for him in this way. Chandramukhi is not a greedy woman now. She tells Devdas that he has lived in her sight neither for the sake of love nor hatred but for 'something', which she has explored in him and which, she can never forget. Her attitude towards life has changed; she herself is totally changed she utters:

> I am not that 'I', I am a bad woman. Do not look at my deficiencies.... I want to live with you. (78)

She becomes very sensitive and wiping her tears reminds him that he has earlier talked about 'woman' who bears stigma, blemish, disgrace, atrocity, aggression, inequity and oppression. she convinces him that after knowing his views about the suffering woman, she has become proud of herself and she has stopped everything. She has learnt to see life in fresh light. We realize the growing spirit of 'new woman' in her. A new enthusiasm has started breathing in her bosom. She is not a slave of male society. Now she is a free woman who can lead a life of her own choice. She has shattered the bondage of prostitute's world—the world of riches, wine and good pass-time to make love business to earn money more and more to fulfil her materialistic desires. Now her journey has started towards spiritualism, goodness gentility, nobility, and cooperation—the qualities, which are never supposed to be found in a so-called prostitute. Now she has experienced the pleasure in 'giving something' instead of 'taking' which she has been practicing in her famous house since long. She proves to be a woman of strong character. She wants to be independent. She talks like a great philosopher and preacher whose inner has brightened. She reports to Dev that she has given up all those objects, which allure and attract man in life. This she has done according to her own wish. Her views lead our soul to soar in the sky higher and higher making an effort and tasting the celestial experience, which she has already realised. We hear such words from the seers in *SATSANG* but soon they start fading gradually with our involvement in materialistic routine. She continues talking like the philosopher of love and differentiates between true love and the business of love. She knows that a man can never understand the sincere heart of a woman who always thinks great about a man. She is cool from outside and the peace is lurking in her eyes. She repeats that she has loved only once and that love is invaluable to her. She clarifies that the love and attraction of beauty are two different things. Man is attracted towards beauty whereas woman sincerely loves but man does not identify it. The lady bears the agony of the soul silently as she has the power to bear. Sincere love is experienced through the depth of the soul, which abounds in peace and satisfaction. She at last wins in convincing Devdas that Parbati has not deceived him but he has deceived himself. She knows that Dev will not understand these things now but the time will tell the truth to him.

Chandramukhi reveals the secrets of woman's heart like an expert psychologist and experienced philosopher. She does not reveal her true love towards Devdas but continues to conceal her love. She expresses that she was pleading on behalf of Parbati, not her. She talks of Sita and Damyanti who are the embodiment of love and sacrifice. It gives an idea of her rich knowledge about Indian classics. She advises him to marry and wishes to pass the rest of her life as a maid in his home. She touches his feet as a reverence and requests him to call her to his aid if he needs. Chandramukhi now is living in a small muddy house located at the bank of the river in Ashthajhari village like a saint. She supports and cooperates needy people and experiences a great pleasure in doing so. One day she expresses her desire to go to Talsonapur village to Bhairav who regarded her with great respect. She anyhow reaches the village of Devdas and tries to know about him and after receiving the right information returns back to start for Calcutta. The altered woman decides with the hope to meet Devdas who is sure to be here in search of peace of heart. She hires a house again in Chitpur area, decorates it, buys the cheap ornaments, gaudy garments so as to give a show of a house of a prostitute. Her hope shatters as Devdas does not turn up for long but one night she discovers a man who is lying down with his face downward. Her heart beat fastens and she recognizes her Deva in spite of darkness all-around. She brings him to her house with a great difficulty and helps him to sleep. Next morning Devdas gets up and finds

Chandramukhi in the same surroundings—the house of a prostitute equipped with alluring objects. He comments:

> Have you started doing all that again? (99)

Who knows about the sacrifice of the great woman! Chandramukhi after all succeeds in her mission—in occupying the seat of love in his heart eliminating hatred. She declares that Devdas is all in all in her life. Devdas has now realised the sincere love of Chandramukhi. He differentiates between his two beloveds and concludes that Parbati is obstinate and strenuous without any blemish on her and unable to bear any kind of aggression whereas Chandramukhi is devoid of self-respect, calm and ready to undergo a stigma, disgrace, atrocity, scoff and condemnation without any sigh on her lips. We realise the height of sacrifice and depth of love of Chandramukhi.

Saratchandra is successful in depicting woman from different strata. Parbati is the symbol of an ordinary woman from middle class society whereas Chandramukhi is that of from lower and defamed class. Saratchandra finds similar hearts beating in the bosom of both the ladies. The repentance of Mrs. Mukharji, the wife of wealthy Zamindar for not marrying Parbati and Devdas and the deserted heart of Parbati's grandmother appeals to our heart and convinces that high or low social status has nothing to do with the sincere love. The journey of the life is diverted from outside world to her inner world. It takes no time to modulate and innovate one's soul. The great saints, preachers and philosophers have turned countless pages of the scriptures to find out the secret of life, which the 'great lady' has learnt in no time. She has crossed the boundaries of materialistic world and has entered in the spiritual and noble world, which is still a dream for many of us. At last I would like to say that Saratchandra's 'Deodas' has the promise of endurance for its sublime factor.

REFERENCE

Saratchandra. 1986. *Deodas.* New Delhi: Subodh Publication.

10

Aap Ka Bunty: A Study in Behavioral Change and Its Motive

ANIL KUMAR SINGH

"Mental processes are essentially unconscious, and that those which are conscious are merely isolated acts and parts of the whole psychic entity." (Freud, Sigmund)

In the realm of Hindi literature, Mannu Bhandari has established herself as a Hindi novelist par excellence with her epoch-making works, *Aap Ka Bunty* (1971) and *Mahabhoj* (1976). She is indeed one of the most renowned of the contemporary Indian woman Hindi novelists. The present Paper is an interpretative psychological study of her *Aap Ka Bunty,* in brief, focusing on the Chief persona, Bunty, which embodies an ironic vision of life in this modern age. In the sense of modernity this is 'the age of Charvak'[1] where human relation is meant to suffer in its own way. Of course, *Aap Ka Bunty* is remarkable for Bunty, the innocent and highly sensitive character who is victim of the divorced and an unadjustable family. Mannu Bhandari has drawn a few canvas characters belonging to middle class society who come across in our day-to-day life indulging themselves sometime for biological urges and sometime for progeny sake.

The novel, *Aap Ka Bunty,* is a problem based novel. Yes, it can also be called a protest novel, a protest against divorce the free biological love and dependence. Yes, it can also be considered as a social satire of the Charvak laden contemporary post-independence Indian society. Mannu Bhandari, with a rare intellectual and artistic ability, is able to create such social pictures that would convey the inexpressible, the complexity of human experiences. In *Aap Ka Bunty*, she expresses successfully the inner and outer rhythms of life, therefore, she is supposed a true and first psychological interpreter of life and ideas, in Hindi literature.

The delineation of Bunty makes us think that Mannu Bhandari has a mastery on child-psychology, she is capable to express the curious nature of Bunty in truthful way because she has a minute and keen observation of child's behaviour. Without any artificiality the character of Bunty has been explored within the novel at some depth with organic relationship with the theme and characters. Like Mulk Raj Anand's (Munnu) coolie, Bunty is shifted from this family to that family but he could not get any blissful place to live in. A nine-year-old child who should live in the lap of mother or in the yard of father is compelled to go to lead a hostel life. Is this the result of cultural decadence or social awakening, a social awakening in the form of individual freedom? Is this the consequence of hidden sexual desire whose bondage is being broken by cultural downfall? If we concentrate on the root cause of such problems. Artificiality in life is the only fountain from where all human problems spring, whether it is problem of divorce or unadjustment or it is a problem of mental agony or alienation, they all are due to lack of 'Knowing' and 'Artificiality'.

Being divorced from Ajay, when Shakun came to live with Dr. Joshi permanently, Dr. Joshi could not bear Bunty as he is often loved and fondled by Shakun. Her prolonged engagement with Bunty is unbearable to Dr. Joshi, as he states to Shakun, "The fondling, kissing and embracing of your mother and son should be stopped now. It seems, you fulfil the urge with Bunty, but you are on right place.... At the end of discourse, there was a hint to (amorous) invitation that made Shakun tickled from outer to inner".[2] Here it is clear that Dr. Joshi is desirous to enjoy the love of Shakun alone. Bunty, naturally, in this way, becomes hindrance in between the two—Shakun and Dr. Joshi.

Bunty, dreamer and 'chief of art club' is more intelligent and highly sensitive than his age. He thinks like an experienced and aged man probably because agony had ripened him before time. Shifting of Shakun's love for Dr. Joshi, is also in the root of shifting attention of Bunty towards Jot, the daughter of Dr. Joshi. This shifting nature of love or hatred is the core of human behaviour. Mannu Bhandari accurately and successfully has observed and shown this human behavioural change. For these reasons probably she concentrates on Bunty chiefly. As it is said, "Child observation is important not only in its own right but also for the insights it can offer into human behaviour generally".[3] Here, I would like to make it clear that my purpose is to trace out the association between the biological processes of mind and body and human behaviour. (But along with this we should remember that psychology covers everything we do).

This novel gets its perfection with the help of various characters like—Ajay, Shakun, Joshi, Bunty, Jot, Ami, Kailash, Titu, Deepak, Aunty, Banshilal etc. The novelist has paid her whole attention and creative power to immortalize Bunty. The relationship between Ajay and Shakun draws readers' attention specially not because of divorce that happened but because of doubt, jealousy, hatred, insincerity and faithlessness in which they led their life for ten years. No doubt, both were facing death in life, both think to get rid of each other, but they don't have in mind about tender and promising Bunty. They could not compromise with their problems, they could not understand each other even in a decade. For their individual happiness, for physical and mental satisfaction they put Bunty in a hostel. But the question is—whether they got real happiness, for which they developed fence all-around in their life, or....? Ajay and Shakun are thinking that divorce is the only solution for procuring tension free life, without caring the future of Bunty. Their divorce brought sadness in Bunti's life. He is in tension, one instance can be seen. "OK. Arup, tell, from where does the Ganga emerge?" Bunty stood up and said, "The Ganga, map, Haridwar, aunty, monkey and papa are now mere names, mere faces, they appear like crowd and everything becomes hotch-potch, everything seems mingled and I cannot tell from where does the Ganga emerge".[4]

What may be the future of Bunty, there is no doubt, Shakun denies the opening sentence of Simone de Beauvoir's *The Second Sex*, "Woman? very simple, say the fanciers of simple formula. She is a womb, an ovary, she is a female. This world is sufficient to define her."[5] The denial in the sense that she challenges to her present miserable situation by divorcing Ajay, the obstinate and brute natured man. Now more and more women have started challenging and questioning patriarchal constructs like family and marriage. There is normalcy on the surface in the life of Shakun even after divorce. She revives herself, her dreams and desires, she wants to quench her physical lust under the love shower of Dr. Joshi. One example is here thought worthy, "Shakun wonders on herself sometime that after crossing the age of 36, she has more and amorous desire like young people. Getting a company of Dr. Joshi she thinks of loneliness and getting loneliness, she thinks...".[6] This emotional flight and sexual desire is no doubt a biological urge which is justified by the character of Shakun. Such human psychology is not kept hidden but is unveiled in its full way. Mannu Bhandari, in describing so, emerges forcefully as a true realist.

In reference to *Aap Ka Bunty*, we must know one thing that Love is more powerful motive than the other motives of human beings. And one thing is also certain that mother loves her children because she sees the glimpse of her husband in them. Bunty is neglected here one by one only because the true father is divorced and neglected. Probably therefore she is ready to send Bunty with Ajay. The same thing also happens with Ajay, the father of Bunty therefore he could not adjust with Bunty and ultimately he was sent to hostel. In case of divorce a woman or a man can live with the help of his or her memory, but after remarriage the previous memories shatter for no-where. Whereas Eckhart Tolle believes, "When you are 'in love' with your partner, this is at first a deeply satisfying state, ...when you are together, you feel whole. The feeling can become so intense that the rest of the world fades into insignificance."[7] Psychologically it seems that Bunty's miserable condition is inflicted by both assumptions.

While in *Aap Ka Bunty*, the role of aunty is popularly known for ideal and religious life. The novelist uses her as a means of superstition and old tradition. She has no applaud for modernity and undue freedom of life. She neither approved the divorce of Ajay and Shakun nor accepted happily the love of Shakun for Dr. Joshi after divorce. She seems extremely furious for such openness and modernity. In a tone of anger, she says,

"In whose house people will leave virtuous track, such thing happens there. It is less happened, more to be happened there now."[8] The character of aunty is woven in a weak and fickle way. Behind such creation, probably Mannu Bhandari might have thought that pseudo idealism is more harmful than naked realism. That is how aunty's expression and presentation is neither forceful nor logical in term of modernity.

Mannu Bhandari believes in describing tension, alienation, mental agony, corruption and frustration of social life. Acclaimed as master piece, *Aap Ka Bunty* is a powerful and poignant study of human relation where there is deep psychological proving, misery and authentic picture of intense mental torture. Like Marx, Freud and Sung have affected and influenced this modern era. Psychological factor plays an important and vital role in modern writing and makes human relation extreme realistic and complete because psychological probing unfold the hidden behaviour—fair or foul—of inner man. The novelist has raised some issues relating the failure of love marriage, divorce and above all the birth of inferiority complex in the mind of a child. In dealing with these issues, she has shown a profound wit and wisdom.

In fact, *Aap Ka Bunty* can be called a milestone and a turning point in the writing of Hindi literature, because of its artistic presentation of human behaviour, especially of child's psychology. Probably through this work Mannu Bhandari has compelled to Hindi writers to think over children even in Charvak dominating society. Really, no Hindi writer reflects so clearly and completely the spirit of child as Mannu Bhandari does in the *Aap Ka Banti.* In her own province, she certainly stands alone. Dr. Mamta Shukla has also accepted rightly, "Mannu Bhandari's *Aap Ka Bunty* unfolds the sharp realities of metropolitan life. This is first novel of Hindi in which a child's mental situation is picturised on a big canvas who is lain in especial circumstances."[9] This novel's story undoubtedly is a journey of human mind which deserves to be kept in mind's paradise forever.

REFERENCES

1. Sotriya Prabhakar. 2003. *Naya Gyanodaya*, Bhartiya Jnanpith, Delhi. 10.
2. Bhandari Mannu. 2000. *Aap Ka Bunty*. New Delhi: Radha Krishna Prakashan. 101.

3. Kristal Leonard. 1979. *Understanding Psychology*. London: Harper and Row. 16.
4. *Aap Ka Bunty* 138.
5. Simonne de Beavoir. 1949. *The Second Sex*, Trans. and Ed. H.M. Parshley. London: Jonathan Cape.
6. *Aap Ka Bunty* 105.
7. Eckhart Tolle. 2001. *The Power of Now*. Mumbai: Yogi Impressions. 124.
8. *Aap Ka Bunty* 99.
9. Mamta Shukla. *Psychological Study of Mannu Bhandari's Fictions*. Ph.D. Thesis at A.P.S. University, Rewa.

11

Pather Panchali, Song of the Road: Bengal's Melody of Life

VIJAY PRAKASH SINGH

It is one of the failings of the publishing industry that though most of us have heard of *Pather Panchali,* the celebrated film by Satyajit Ray not many of us outside Bengal know that the film was based on a classic of Bangla literature. First serialized in the journal *Vichitra* the novel was published in book form in 1929. It has run into six editions which include two abridged versions for children.

It is only befitting that Harper Collins should have brought out an English edition in 1999 sub-titled *Song of the Road.*[1] This edition is a translation of the Bangla original by T.W. Clark and Tarapada Mukherji, both teachers of Bengali at the school of Oriental and African studies at the University of London.

Clark and Mukherji's translated narrative is never contrived or unnatural. It has a lucid authenticity that would appeal to a wide readership. This is in great measure due to the authenticity of the original novel and the spontaneity of its narrative. As Clark points out:

> The immediate appeal of *Pather Panchali,* which the passage of time has done nothing to weaken can in the main be attributed to two factors; first its vivid, moving and utterly authentic portrayal of village people and their day-to-day life; secondly the fact that the subject was presented through the minds, eyes and lips of a small boy and his sister, Opu and Durga. (11)

Pather Panchali has two parts: Part 1 is entitled *The Old Aunt* and Part 2 *Children Make Their Own Toys.* While the thrust of the book is on the childhood of the siblings Opu and Durga, the portrayal of the ostracized widow Indir Thakrun as the old aunt is no less poignant.

Indir Thakrun is Horihor's distant aunt from his mother's side. Horihor is the father of Opu and Durga. Indir Thakrun is a widow and has no one to support her nor a home of her own. She has hardly had a decent married life even when her husband a Kulin Brahmin was alive:

> Kulins were notorious for multiple marriages and Indir's husband who apparently had many wives, seldom came to visit her. On a few occasions he did come, he stayed no more than a night or two, and after collecting all the money which custom decreed to be his due, he ticked off the village in his book and went with his coolie to the next village he had married into. (6)

Indir Thakrun has been a destitute virtually all her life, dependent upon her parents and after their death on her brother and finally on Horihor. She lives in a thatched hut in a corner of Horihor's compound and because Horihor had barely enough to feed his own family, her presence irks his wife Shorbojoya who quarrels with her on the slightest pretext. Durga is very fond of the old woman, hearing stories from her and even shielding her from her mother's virulent attacks on the old woman. Shorbojoya unable to bear the old woman as it is, becomes jealous of her because of her daughter's loyalty to her.

> She called her an old witch and a vampire because she was convinced that Durga was fonder of the old woman than she was of her mother. She was jealous and very angry to think that the child of her womb was being estranged from her. (33)

Tired of Shorbojoya's insults Indir Thakrun often leaves her house wrapping up her few possessions in a bundle and takes off for the forest. She seeks new shelters and is provided hospitality for a few days after which 'as the weeks went past her welcome began to wear thin' (42) and she returns to Horihor's house. After one such skirmish when she is hounded out by Shorbojoya, she falls ill and starvation, fever, old age and the sorrow of being treated like a pariah culminate in her death. She dies as she has lived, like an outcast, unwanted and unloved. She dies before the last rite of pouring the holy water of the Ganges can be performed and from 'the sunken sockets tears welled out and flowed down her cheeks' (48).

In a book essentially detailing the joys and hidden pleasures of childhood it seems incongruous that the writer should have chosen to portray the traumas of old age. The incongruity is no longer of any account when we remind ourselves that the only person who treats Indir like a human being, with love and kindness, is Durga. The innocence of childhood bonds with the vulnerability of old age. Children bond with adults in the same way as they do with other children, with a friendliness that is irrespective of the person's status or wealth. Indir's suffering at the hands of Shorbojoya has also, as Clark suggests, a Karmic significance. The suffering that Shorbojoya heaps on Indir becomes in the course of time her own relentless privation: poverty to the point of starvation, Durga's death and in *Aparajito* the sequel to *Pather Panchali* the loss of her husband and when Opu leaves for school and college her struggles with poverty and loneliness. Indir's plight can also be seen as a social documentation of the suffering that widowhood in Bengal entailed in a chauvinist, male-oriented society that decreed an end to all material comforts and often an end to social status, respect and even human dignity for the widow.

Part 2 of the book entitled *Children make their own toys* is the real flavour and rhythm of *Pather Panchali.* Horihor and Shorbojoya's children Opu and Durga are children born and brought up in impoverished circumstances. Leave alone enjoying the special privileges of childhood or any of its luxuries the siblings subsist on a poor diet, 'of rice and stringy root vegetables or unflavoured, boiled pumpkin' (156).

Yet despite such crippling poverty, life's treasure-house of joys and thrills is full to the brim for Opu and Durga. Their childhood is an unbroken series of truants, mischievous adventures and sudden escapades. They seem to be always in pursuit of some new thrill: be it stealing mangoes or having a secret picnic in a deserted compound, playing with cowrie shells, adding odds and ends to the doll box or running off to see a train or the *Jatra*. The monotony of life is broken by the several festivals of rural Bengal in which Shorbojoya with her limited resources cooks delicacies for the children.

Opu and Durga are children of the forest. Nature in all her pristine glory with its shaded bamboo groves, flowering creepers and birds beckons to them and they eagerly seek its fascinating bounties. All their joy and sense of wonder and enchantment stem from the forest. They cherish a sylvan childhood with an ever renewing zest. They never grow tired of the forest nor seek the urban distractions missing from village life.

> This forest with its freshness and deep green shadows had laid its fingers on Opu and his sister alike, and had brought peace and consolation into their hearts. They had known it all their lives. Day by day, hour by hour, its silence and its delights poured rich and varied nectars into their thirsting souls.... The wonder and ever-changing joys of the forest filled Opu with emotions which are too deep for words. (169)

Much later after Durga's death during his first pilgrimage to Ganganandpur Opu reflects on his bond with nature:

> Day by day as the years of his childhood passed, Opu walked with nature... his heart leaped within him to behold the seasons touching the changing face of the Ichamoti with new beauties. (332)

The seemingly endless trysts with nature and the wonderful companionship of Opu and Durga stretch in episode after episode until the tragic turn in the novel with the death of Durga.

Sometime before her death, Durga begins to have a premonition that 'something was going to happen to her, and that it was going to happen soon' (229). Uncannily this sense of something imminent clings to her with a tenacity, 'The fear like a dreadful savage beast dogged her wherever she went and whatever she did'. There seemed to be no escaping it. Durga's intuition is realized when she contracts malaria and begins to suffer from a fever. As if in conspiracy with her slow death by malaria the elements of nature conjure up a theatre of destructive frenzy like the dance of Shiva. The monsoon rain pours in torrents, uprooting trees, breaking down Shorbojoya's hut and leaving her virtually on the brink of disaster, a victim of penury starvation and Durga's unabating fever:

> There was nothing to see: no sky, no tree, no cloud, no movement, no night even, only black nothingness, opaque and impenetrable; blackness peopled by hordes of demons, who snarled about her like beasts of prey and gnashed at her with their teeth, invisibly. Who could they be but minions and precursors of the ultimate destroyer, as they rushed inexorably on with terror and diabolical speed to consummate their universal destruction.... (286)

In a climax of relentless deluge of rain the malaria and starvation takes its toll on Durga and she languishes away to death. Horihor returns after this tragic loss only to be told by his wife that Durga is no more. This is the most poignant part of Bandhopadhyay's idyllic narrative. All the hopes and joys, all the pranks and laughter of childhood come to an end with young Durga's death. Life goes on for Opu, distracted as he is by the daily diversions of the village but the void left behind by Durga's death rankles him later when he is leaving Nischindpur:

> The red flowers in the hedge reminded him of her.... The only living creature to whom he could run and share his pleasures had gone away and left him.... And she would never, never come back and play with him again. (347)

The departure from Nischindpur marks a turning point in the life of Opu who has never seen a train, leave alone travelled in one. He is sad at leaving Nischindpur due to its countless associations but being the child that he is, he is also full of a curious thrill at the unknown life he and his parents are embarking upon. Significantly thoughts of Durga return to him as the train leaves Nischindpur and he remembers how her last wish had been to see a train:

> They had not brought her with them, they had all come away and left her behind. Though she had been dead for a long time now, he had always felt her near him.... Every corner in their dilapidated old house in Nischindpur still spoke to him of her loving though invisible presence; and now he was being parted from her for ever. (357)

With Opu's loving thoughts of his sister and the gnawing loss of her death, *Pather Panchali* comes full circle: death in old age repeats itself as death in youth. It is a *fin de siecle*. Death, penury and privation alternate with the innumerable small joys of life in a rhythm that is unfathomable to man. This rhythm is, as the writer shows us, the only reality of life that is unshakeable, timeless and universal.

The landscape of Bengal with its lush profusion and its rivers, its vibrant festivals and its traditional customs and the stronghold of its caste hierarchy is very much a part of the story of *Pather Panchali*, placing the novel in its specific social and cultural context.

In its heart-rending depiction of Indir Thakrun's widowed old-age and its exuberant evocation of the joy's of childhood there are few novels in the canons of Classical literature that could compare with *Pather Panchali*. Satyajit Ray's film is a monumental tribute to the genius of Bibhutibhushan Bandhopadhyay but it has passed into the archives of cinematic connoisseurship. It is the novel that deserves a resurrection—outside Bengal—from the oblivion to which it had fallen. The translated edition which is evidently a labour of love on the part of T.W. Clark and Tarapada Mukherji will go a long way towards this end.

REFERENCE

1. Bibhutibhushan Bandhopadhyay. 2001. *Pather Panchali*. Trans. by T.W. Clark and Tarapada Mukherji. New Delhi: Harper Collins.

12

Masti and Basheer: Story-tellers from the South

VIJAY PRAKASH SINGH

Masti was born on June 6, 1891 in a Brahmin family. His childhood and adolescence were marked by poverty and death. He received his B.A. from Central College, Bangalore and was awarded a Gold medal for standing First at the M.A. examination at Madras University. He joined the Civil Service as Assistant Commissioner, Excise. Subsequently he started his literary career with the publication of a collection of short-stories in Kannada entitled *Kelavu Sanna Kathegalu*. Thereafter began a prolific writing career which culminated with the publication of *Chikaveera Rajendra* for which he received the Jnanpeeth Award.

Katha publications has brought out a translation of Masti Venkatesh Iyengar's short-stories drawn from his various collections in Kannada in 1995. Masti has a simplicity of style that the translator Ramchandra Sharma has retained in English. There is an immediacy of voice in the narration that effectively conveys the purpose of each story. Most stories are, as the writer makes clear at the onset, retold narratives. This true or assumed retelling of a story is a style that some of the masters of the art of story-telling like Henry James and Somerset Maugham have used to suggest rather than define or explain a particular situation. The second-hand narrative often ends in ambiguity with the writer offering scant explanation for why or how the story has taken the turn that it does. The most everyday events—unlike James or Maugham's stories—make up the content of Masti's fiction as in *Ranga's Marriage* and *Our Teacher.*

On the other hand stories like *An Old Tale, An Unfortunate Woman* and *A Tale Told by Gouthami* are based on the eternal theme of sexual passions and the ambivalent nature of human sexuality. In *An Old Tale* a *sanyasi* is strongly drawn to a young woman who spends the night in his shelter. His desire for the woman sleeping next to his room conflicts with the ascetics life he has chosen and he is in turmoil. Yet he denies the presence of the desire. Theoretically the *sanyasi* believes that ascetics transcend their sexual desires. To vindicate this belief the *sanyasi* goes to the extent of altering the text of Vyasa's *shloka* in which he says that "a woman's beauty is sure to attract every man, be he old or wise, or a *sanyasi*" (42). The *sanyasi* makes his disciple alter the *shloka* to suit his theory so that us reads, "A woman's beauty is sure to attract old man, and the wise man. But never a *sanyasi*." Yet despite nurturing this belief in the sexual detachment of the ascetic life the *sanyasi* find himself in the throes of desire. His desire is compelling as long as he resists it. He is so overwhelmed by the woman sleeping in the adjoining room that he insists that she open the door for him. When the woman refuses he pushes the door open only to have a vision of Vyasa, his face glowing with the power that comes from years of meditation (54). Vyasa startles the *sanyasi* with the bitter truth of his statement, "You weren't attracted to her and yet you madly desired to see her face", he says. The truth dawns on the *sanyasi* and he begs the sage's forgiveness saying "I am a great sinner" (54). He realizes that the truth of sexual desire cannot be denied but it can be surmounted in a spirit of surrender to God.

An Old Tale is a powerful story and it must rank amongst the best that Masti wrote. Its similarity to Somerset Maugham's story *Rain* should be obvious to anyone who has read that masterpiece by Maugham. In *Rain* a vicar tries hard to reform a prostitute but instead falls prey himself to her seduction and commits suicide. Maugham is a realist, predominantly concerned with human fallibility. Masti on the other hand belongs to a culture where asceticism and self-abnegation has been a centuries-old tradition. It is this ascetic tradition to which Masti pays tribute in *An Old Tale.*

Much like *An Old Tale* published in 1920 Masti wrote *A Tale Told by Gouthami* published nearly three decades later in 1947. The situation is reversed in Gouthami with a young woman caught up in the throes of desire for a *sanyasi* who spurns her advances. The young man whom Malini loves drowns in a river and when the pain of his loss begins to fill up she finds herself hankering for his friend Datta who had withdrawn from her despite his love for her when he realizes that she loves his friend Bhardwaj and not him. With the passing of time Datta attains such a level of spiritual discipline that he is widely respected. Love and desire are a thing of the past for him. For Malini, Bhardwaj's death is a thing of the past and her unfilled desire due to his death can only look to Datta for consummation. Masti's delineation of Malini as a woman who asserts her sexuality in a male-oriented society and seeks sexual consummation from a *sanyasi* is bold to say the least. For a story published in 1947 it is also ahead of its time. Malini first propose to Datta that they should get married but Datta refuses saying, "You became my sister-in-law and I have looked upon you as such ever since. I can't think of you as my wife now" (160). A year later Malini becomes so bold as to propose to Datta that they should live together as lovers even if they do not get married. Datta reasons with Malini and appeals to her, "though younger in years, you are older in wisdom. So take me by the hand and lead me on the right path" (164). Despite this appeal Malini, blinded with desire "lunged at him with outstretched arms, wanting to grab his face and pull it towards her breasts" at which Datta once again pleads with her, "You are a woman, Adishakti the primeval force. There's nothing like a fall for you. I am a man. I can never hope to keep my soul pure. It's only with your blessing that I can hope to succeed. If you are adamant, I will lose my way. Bless me, I beg you, and save me" (164). Like the *sanyasi* in *An Old Tale*, Malini realizes her folly and "her virtuousness came to her rescue at that moment" (164). *A Tale Told by Gouthami* is an original story in that it explores the fact that a woman's sexuality can be as compelling as that of a man's. Like *An Old Tale, A Tale Told by Gouthami* emphasizes the idea of sexual restraint as a necessary requisite to attain spiritual enlightenment.

An Unfortunate Woman published in 1949 is about a young girl married to an impotent man. The impotent man lures the girl to marrying him so that he can use her as a prostitute to live of her earnings. The girl resists the idea in the beginning but when she reflects on the alternative she has of returning to her parental home she decides to accept the prostitutes life to fulfil her desires. Amongst several of her clients there is one with whom she falls in love. She asks this man to persuade her husband to give her up but the husband is so angry at the idea that he threatens to call the police. A violent altercation ensues in which the woman's lover murders the husband. The murderer is caught but in the court proceedings against him he is acquitted because his act is seen "as a case of causing death with no malice aforethought" (150). *An Unfortunate Woman* is a bizarre story of the debasement to which human nature can fall. Like *A Tale Told by Gouthami,* it shows the unconventional side of the woman's sexuality. As the wife of an impotent man the young girl make the choice of prostituting herself rather than living a sexually unfulfilled life.

Masti wrote of the everyday concerns and the serious preoccupations of men and women in a style that is most unassuming and spontaneous. It would be interesting to see how a contemporary of his in nearby Kerala was giving expression to his vision of life in another language. This contemporary was Vaikom Basheer Mohammed (1908-1994) who wrote in Malyalam. Basheer was born on January 20, 1908 in the village of Thalayolaparambu in Vaikom (Travancore district). He attended the Malyalam school in Thalayolaparambu and later the Vaikom English School. Basheer participated in the Salt Satyagraha at Calicut in April 1930 for which he was arrested and then tortured in various lockups. When he was released from jail, he joined *Ujjevanam,* a paper which promoted terrorism. When the police seized his anti-British writings, he left Kerala. He wandered all over India for the next seven years until he reached the shores of Arabia. His first story, *Ente Thankam* was published in *Jayakesari,* a weekly. He earned fame as a writer with the publication of his novella *Balyakalasakhi* in 1944. During the years 1947-48 he worked as a journalist on the editorial boards of several Malayali periodicals amongst which was *Jayakeralam* in Madras. He returned from Madras and started a bookstall called Circle Book House in Ernakulam which he changed later to the new name, Basheer's Book Stall. During the years 1953-58 after suffering a psychological setback Basheer underwent treatment at Ayurveda Mental Clinic, Trichur. In 1981 he received the Kerala Sahitya Akademi Fellowship again, the Padma Shri was conferred on him in 1982. For the next over one decade he received several awards within Kerala such as the *Lalithambika Antharajanam* and the *Vallathol Puraskaram*. Basheer passed away on July 5, 1994.

Katha has brought out a translation of Basheer's representative short stories in 1996. Basheer is a master of satire. In stories like *The Card-Sharper's Daughter* originally published as *Mucheetukalikkarante Makal* in 1951 and in *Mantara Charatu* published in 1975, Basheer shows us the craftiness that human nature is capable of. In *The Card-Sharper's Daughter* Ottakkannan Pokker's daughter Zainaba cheats her own father so that she can marry Mandan Mathapa the man who courts her. Similarly in *Mantara Charatu* a conman sells amulets for various diseases which gullible people like Abdul Aziz and his wife Ummusalma buy. These stories with their element of satire have some of the lightness of R.K. Narayan's fiction. Narayan's stories like *An Astrologer's Day* and *A Horse and Two Goats* have a similar element of irony as in Basheer's stories. These stories of irony and satire lead one to stories of the absurd suh as *The World-renowned Nose* published as *Vishwavikhyatamaya Mookku* in an anthology of the same name in 1954 and *Ettukali Mammoonhu* published in 1967. In these stories the incredible is depicted as caricature. In *The World-renowned Nose* a character named Mookken develops a nose that goes down to his navel and he becomes the cynosure of all eyes and then a pawn amidst conflicting political lobbies. In *Ettukali Mammoonhu*, the main character of the story is called Ettukali because he looks like a spider. He is short-statured with a small head and a one-foot long mustache that hung on either side of his face. Such incredibly quaint physical attributes give to Basheer's stories an element of the fairy-tale. Irony, satire and caricature all combine to produce a fiction that teases the logical reader's credulity while it amuses. It is a surrealist fiction that draws from the bizarre rather than from mundane reality. It engages the reader's attention as long as the story lasts but hardly makes a lasting impact like some of Masti's stories do. Masti takes mundane life of human nature as his raw material and works it into stories of memorable appeal. Yet it would be wrong to evaluate Basheer only on the basis of his stories of satire or caricature.

In stories like *Walls* originally published as *Mathilukal* in 1965 and *Voices* originally published as *Sabdangal* in 1947 Basheer shows the existentialist side of his fiction. Voices could be the expression of any man alienated from the mainstream of society: a man who doesn't know who his parents are, what his religion is, a man who does not want to conform to social conventions and has become a nameless pariah. This man represents sexual depravity; he has fornicated with prostitutes as a result of which he suffers from gonorrhea. His narrative is an incoherent rambling that has no direction until the point when he attempts suicide but ironically fails just as he has failed to make any sense of his life. *Voices* in Basheer's existentialist expression of despair but in placing the story of his character's life in a specific predicament he confuses the reader who is left wondering if the character's despair is meant to suggest the general human condition or whether the purpose of the writer is merely to depict the psychology of a pariah. The rambling nature of the narrative with its frequent shifts of situation in which the narrator's hopelessness is reinforced does not help the reader in making sense of the writer's purpose.

Mathilukal published nearly two decades later than *Sabdangal* in 1965 shows far greater focus of style. The protagonist is a prisoner who relieves the tedium of prison life by gardening and nurturing his sexual desires for the women prisoner's who live on the other side of his own prison walls. The women are never revealed but their presence is suggested throughout the story by the compulsive fantasy of male desire. The prisoner in the story indulges in a fantasy about a woman who seems to be the creation of his imagination. Yet the specific details of this woman prisoner make her very real. Her name is Narayani and she is twenty-two years old. The male prisoner's courtship with Narayani brings out his utter desolation. *Mathilukal* is narrated with a conviction because it is based on the experience of Basheer's own life in prison.

One of the finest stories in the Katha translation of Basheer's stories is *The rightful inheritors of the earth* originally published as *Bhoomiyute Avakasikal* published in 1946. This simply told story carries a social message that is perhaps far more relevant today. It is a story that questions man's presumption that he is the master of the universe when in fact the vast variety of animals in nature have as much claim to the fruits of nature as man. The ecological relevance of this story written nearly six decades ago makes it one of the finest in the collection.

It is clear from a study of the stories of Basheer that he inhabits a very different world from the one, which Masti wrote about. While Basheer wrote of deception, guile, fantasy, alienation and sexual depravity Masti wrote of restraint, sacrifice and Puritanism. Basheer writes of the negative emotions that he has been witness to while Masti tempers even overwhelming emotions like sexual desire by his morality. While Basheer is a realist, Masti is a moralist. On the other hand in terms of form whereas Basheer experiments with fantasy and surrealism, Masti never deviates from the traditional narrative. What is common to both writers is their abiding humanism, their faith in the values of strong character and their disregard of all that is debasing in human nature. Both writers spring from a southern socio-cultural ethos and have come down to us as non-Kannada and non-Malyali readers, reading their stories in English as powerful voices to reckon with. A multi-dimensional universality of concerns marks the writing of both story-tellers and one wishes that other publishers as enterprising as Katha bring out translations of the major works of Masti and Basheer for readers in English to discover.

REFERENCES

1. Venkatesha Iyengar. 1995. *Masti Short Stories.* Translated and Edited by Ramchandra Sharma. New Delhi: Katha.
2. Muhammad Basheer. 1996. *Vaikom Short Stories* Edited by Vanajam Ravindran. New Delhi: Katha.

13

WARRING IMPULSES: A STUDY OF PRATIBHA RAY'S *TRANSGRESSION* (AN ORIYA SHORT STORY IN TRANSLATION)

NEELANJAN PATHAK

> "Virtue that transgresses is but patched with sin's and sin that amends is but patched with virtue."
>
> (Shakespeare—*Twelfth Night* Act 1 Sc. V/52)

The contribution of regional writers to Indian writings is momentous because it is in their writings that the plural population of the country finds its authentic representation. Indeed their writings unfold only small sections of our varied culture, but these ultimately weave themselves to reveal the spirit of the sub-continent. A translation of some of the best of these stories into English has gained critical acceptability inaugurating a new chapter in Indian fiction in English. Short stories by Anita Desai, Jhumpa Lahiri, Margaret Mascarenas, Nayantara Sehgal (apart from the many regional writers) have turned the eyes of the world to the stories written by women. Women writers are largely successful in photographing the traumas of women of India who have for ages been living as the weaker sex—'the Other', 'the subalterns' to use contemporary terms. Every part of India with its distinguishing ambience provides to a regional writer a perspective for capturing the pulse of the nation. R.K. Narayana acknowledges in his essay 'The Problem of the Indian Writer' that the short story is popular here with fiction writers not only because it takes less time, but because it can adapt itself to the "Variegated material available in the country" (15).

The paper is designed as an analysis of an Oriya short story "Ullanghan" by Pratibha Ray who is a representative voice of Orissa—a fiction writer, a critic, a translator and an educationist. She has worked as a Reader of Education and presently on deputation to the Orissa Public Service Commission. She focuses primarily on issues related to women and the tribal communities of Orissa. One of her well-known novels is *Yajnasani* (1985) which won her the prestigious Moorti Devi award. She was honoured by the Orissa Sahitya Akademi award for her short story collection *Ullanghan and Other Stories*. The little piece of this work has been translated by another eminent Oriya writer Bikram K. Das under the title *Transgression*. Translator Das is also an Akademy award winner whose rendering of this story interprets the non-English mind-set intact into English making the translation process seamless. In this paper, an attempt shall be made to articulate the predicaments and warring impulses that stare the protagonists. This story set in a village ruled by orthodox modes of behaviour, examines the nuances of a less conventional man-woman relationship—that between a father-in-law and a daughter-in-law. Ray observes through her fictional magnifying lens the quandary faced by a woman who has conditioned her existence according to the demands of duty. My point of view is entirely individual—while convergence with the ideas expressed would be highly satisfying, divergence too would be equally esteemed for it will lead to a deeper insight into a subject that can be variously interpreted.

Before attempting an analysis it would be worthwhile to present a thumbnail sketch of the story. It opens with the male protagonist. Bhabanath nostalgically reliving the memories of his young age. Deeply inspired by the Vedantic philosophy of belief in the infinite as the only reality, Bhabanath had spent his youthful years in service of the family deity at the 'thakurbadi'. His holy ways of life had earned him the veneration of people of ten neighbouring villages. It was only in his father's desire that he had married Savitri (who is a devoted wife) to carry on the family lineage. Theirs was a home built not on traditions of love, but of service. Savitri lived neglected and silent and when she died her life was thought complete because she had given birth to a son and had died with vermilion and the 'Odhana' on her head. Bhabanath believed it was weak on the part of man to shed a tear of sorrow impressing the awe-struck villagers by his stoicism. History repeated itself as his son, Srinath grew up in awe of his father, who had remained a widower the rest of his life completely dedicated to his ideals of asceticism. When he married Manju, the female protagonist in the story, she was repeatedly instructed that her prime role lay in serving her father-in-law. Unquestioningly, for years as Srinath remained out on transfer, Manju continued to live with her father-in-law whose love she had earned through her selfless ways. An unparalleled emotional bond ties the two together as Manju becomes an emblem of an ideal daughter-in-law in the eyes of all villagers. During the evening of his life Bhabanath begins to see an image of his own neglected wife in Manju. Gradually, seeds of passion start gaining entrance in Bhabanath's disturbed psyche. One day as Manju was massaging his feet; he holds her hands firmly and tells her that they are very much like her mother-in-law's. In the turning point of the story, one night Manju is stupefied on finding Bhabanath in her lampless room. His pretext is that he had lost his way to the toilet. Manju loses all peace of mind, her letters to her husband continued, only to instruct her not to fail in her duties. Finally, when a second time she is startled at night by a groping hand, she takes the momentous decision. Next morning, she leaves the house and the dependent old man, not to return till his death, unmindful of the reproofs of the villagers and the anger of her husband. Manju never offered an explanation for her at of turning away from her responsibility because her husband had always believed that "All destruction has its origin in a woman's brain" (44). Ray ends the story leaving it on the discretion of her reader whether Manju's decision was justified or not. We are not told who is the transgressor.

The *Webster's Dictionary* defines transgression as—stepping across; 'breaching a limit or boundary', and acting in violation of law. In the *Oxford Dictionary* it is defined as 'going beyond the limit of what is morally or legally acceptable' or 'offending against a moral principle'. In view of these, it will now be considered who is the transgressor and what are the conditions that may have led to transgression. Fiction has always considered both the positive and negative angles of human temperament as they reveal themselves in inter-personal relationships. Ray's appeal lies here in the convincing portrayal of an exalted relationship degenerating into an incredibly base motive. Both Manju and Bhabanath end up as human beings who invariably fall into error when guided by impulses. Obliquely, the short story hints how crucial it is to be continuously conscious of our limits in order to retain a stainless conscience.

An Indian woman's identity is almost always examined in relationship with a man—she is a wife, a sister, a mother, a beloved or like Manju a daughter-in-law. She is close to the picture of woman expressed by the thinker Jean Jacques Rousseau of existing only to be sweet, pleasing and agreeable to man. Indian wives have been symbols of idealised virtue. Both Savitri and Manju exist not as individuals but as shadows of their male counterparts without any glimpse of selfhood in them. How often in India, wives live separated for years from their husbands because they are more needed to serve the husband's family. Manju is revealed primarily as nurse to her father-in-law, meekly obeying the instructions of her husband. She reminds one of the loneliness of Urmila, the legendary wife of Lakshman in *The Ramayana*, who had lived away from her husband for fourteen long years. In upholding the ideals imposed upon wives, Manju stands as tall as her sisters from Indian mythology like Sita and Savitri. Her character is portrayed dispassionately by the writer, without any trace of sentimentalism, so that there is an unimpeded sense of immediacy in the story.

Towards the climax of the story, Manju who had always silenced the voice of the angst within is led by circumstances to redefine her role. She stands at a crossroad where one option is to continue to live on in spite of understanding the rise of carnal desires in her father-in-law and thereby keep up her social image and the other more intimidating option is to be unmindful of all social codes and respond only to the voice of the Self within. By choosing the latter, she evolves in one brief moment through her few short steps taken to cross the thresholds of a house, which allows her no shelter. Borrowing from the feminist critic Elaine Showalter's modern theory of phases of feminism, she steps from the feminine phase of acceptance of tradition to the Feminist Phase of protest. Effacement of identity she had all along endured, but she would not endure infringement of virtue. Manju proves that a submissive woman may not always be synonymous with a weak woman—she cannot be taken for granted. Years of subservience had not clouded Manju's ability to take a self-supporting decision during a crucial predicament.

Had Manju decided to stay on, she would have transgressed in her role as a wife. Unlike a staunch feminist who breaks the chrysalis of family only to prove her own identity, Manju did not step out in defiance or rebellion. Her decision of leaving is her only means of living up her own sense of morality. The cacophony within had turned unendurable so she had to turn deaf to social reproaches. By turning her back to her duties, as a daughter-in-law Manju did not transgress—rather, she prevents Bhabanath from transgressing before reaching a point of no return. She is the victimized who is helplessly driven to cross a threshold where she has ungrudgingly witnessed the erosion of all her youthful dreams and the frittering away of her innermost desires. The writer is aware that compression is the key to the success of a short story so her focus is only on those aspects, which contribute in one way or another to the unfolding of the story's plot. We are not allowed direct glimpses into Manju's emotions—they are only suggested.

Though the persona of Bhabanath Ray shows us the discord that is a natural outcome of conflicting ideas. To borrow Hindi idioms in his there is a dichotomy of a 'yogi' and a 'bhogi'. During his youth Bhabanath had curbed worldly pleasures as lust playing "hide and seek with life and truth" (39). Although theoretically he had believed that renunciation was greater than indulgence, he could not entirely tame his desires while living within the framework of family. The ordeals of self-discipline require one to spend years in seclusion away from all worldly enticements. At the sunset of life, as Bhabanath's suppressed cravings surface, he ends up as a failure in both his roles—neither can he be an ascetic nor a contented human being. His fall in the end is very steep because all along his virtues and nobility had raised him to a very high pedestal. When a demi-god like character gradually harbours unlawful thoughts towards a daughterly daughter-in-law, he not only becomes a transgressor but a sinner. The demon of desire had revealed its ugly face "when bone and flesh were in decay" (48). Bhabanath is a transgressor because he could not triumph over his negative instincts. His frailty proved that in spite of commanding the awe of so many around himself, at heart Bhabanath had been lonely and incomplete without a woman to fulfil his emotional and physical needs. The translator's veracity in conveying the ideas exactly in the English version may be substantiated by this brief citation: "when gold is firm, it conceals all dross, but when it melts the dross is exposed" (45).

If Manju can be compared with Sita or Urmila, Bhabanath becomes comparable with Dashrath, King of Ayodhya. Indian epics are filled with events that are a consequence of transgression. To cite a few instances, Dashrath, an ideal king and a husband who kept his word to Kaikeyi transgresses as a father in sending Ram to exile for no fault of his. Rama, the very paragon of virtue transgresses as a husband in commanding site to go through the fire ordeal. Even Krishna, transgresses as a warrior in using unfair means to assist Bhim in killing Duryodhana. Both fiction and life have made it explicit that mortals come to grief because of ignorance of their limits in the sundry roles that they need to play. In the Indian scenario, women live in conformity with unwritten laws that often compel them to accept that they are wrong even when they are actually the wronged ones. Without sounding didactic, Ray exposes this fact of society as may be evident through his statements from the story. Regarding Bhabanath her opinion is that "He seemed to be possessed by some evil spirit, determined to destroy all trust, morality tradition" (45). Despite this the verdict against Manju is unambiguous "The reproofs of the entire village poured over her in a flood" (46).

Bhabanath is however not an unredeemed sinner, but a complex fictional persona portrayed through astute psychological insight. In his devoted and caring daughter-in-law he had for years been seeing a picture of his wife who he had always neglected. This attraction towards Manju begins with a helpless realisation of his inadequacy as a husband.

There is an undercurrent of deep pathos bringing him close to a classical tragic hero, in his last prayer :

> God give me back my youth. Return my Savitri to me. Restore my strength. I want to taste life as a normal being. (46)

Physically, a tottering shadow of his former self, at this juncture he is faced with existential anxieties that he is unable to fight against. As he recapitulates Manju becomes not only an icon of his dead wife, but also a symbol of youth and fertility, which he now lacks. Therefore, "the stealthy touch of a groping hand" that had startled Manju could only have been a semi-conscious move by an insecure man to verify whether Manju actually existed in human form or was she a vision of Savitri's spirit.

In writing of *Transgression* Ray is certainly not experimenting with a new theme. Even the *Bible* mentions transgression by mortals as an affliction to the Lord: "But he was wounded for our transgression". What is new is the covert ambiguity. To both the protagonists, existence does not remain the same once ethical boundaries have been traversed. Proverb fifteen from *The Bible* says, "The way of transgressors is hard". Bhabanath dies an aggrieved man while Manju lives under the oppression of her husband's blame and social censure. As an omniscient narrator Ray explores the innermost recesses of Bhabanath's mind in his degeneration from a saint to a sinner.

According to the literal implication of the work 'transgression' Bhabanath transgressor the moment he enters the daughter-in-law's room with an immoral thought while Manju transgresses by crossing the threshold where duty had necessitated her to live for years. Metaphorically, Bhabanath's transgression lies in the violation of the sanctity of a relationship while Manju's transgression is in deserting an old man who is entirely dependent on her. The question raised by the author is pertinent: "If those feet standing at death's door had stumbled, could she not steady them with her strong hands?"(49). Ray provides no cut and dried answer. In Manju's decision we discover the 'brave new woman' who is gradually emerging in spite of the many impediments that stand tall before her. Every account of female predicament enriches our own perception of the long subjection of Indian womanhood, which is so much a part of our tradition.

Ray's story is rooted in indigenous ethos and could only have been written by an Indian writer. Not only are the characters very close to our everyday acquaintances, but even the situation is not hypothetical. The interplay between innate desires and external behaviour provoke the readers to think for long after the story is closed. It reminds one of Frank O' Connor's words that a short story "must plummet to the bottom of the mind" (216). It is a story which fuses exposure of conventional social behaviour with the pathos of the victimized, the marginalised the woman who forms part of that population of our country where the talk of woman's emancipation will take years to reach. Pratibha Ray's novels and short stories usually depict the urbane milieu of Orissan culture and the life of tribal communities, but to appreciate her comprehension of elemental passions that govern the human mind, one needs to turn to this remarkable.

14

CHITRA MUDGAL'S *BEAST*: A POINT OF VIEW

SHOBHA DIWAKAR

She is a Hindi novelist, short story writer and journalist. She has written more than 16 books, including books for children. She has received many awards including, the Hindi Sahitya Academi Award twice.

This is a tragic story written by Chitra Mudgal and translated from the original Hindi version by Deepa Agarwal who is also an Indian English poet and short story writer who also writes for children and has a dozen books to her credit. She received the Asian Age Short Story Competition Award in 1995.

Before I commence further I would like to acknowledge that the name of the story in Hindi is not known to me. This is a translation that I came across in the Sahitya Akademi's Bi-Monthly Journal No. 210: Vol. 46, No. 4 published July-Aug. 2002 from New Delhi. I would also like to add that my study is restricted strictly to the text and the opinions expressed are entirely my own.

The story in question is very simple. The plot moves round a poor tongawala and his sickly horse, Sarwa. The theme revolves round the tongawala's deep concern over his sick horse and the urge to earn money for his almost starving family. The guilty conscience that strikes the tongawala towards the end of the story and the spiritual crisis he passes through brings about its catastrophe and also its denouncement.

The narrative opens on a scorching summer's day when the tongawalla, Aslam is hailed by five burqua-clad women, accompanied by four children. Looking sadly at his sick and frail horse he realizes distressingly how impossible it would be for her (Sarwa) to pull nine people. He is lost in his thoughts; reflecting that if he demanded ten rupees, the women would spare him. However, after some haggling the women agree and he finds himself cornered. Five hefty women with two babes on their hips are followed by two other who seat themselves contentedly in the Tonga. It is when Sarwari makes and endeavour to lift and move her legs forward that Aslam realizes that she is oppressed by the weight of its passengers and is barely able to pull along the Tonga. A minute before he had thought. I quote:

> Wont the loads of nine people drain everything from her?
>
> No, he didn't want to finish her off completely.

(Indian Literature, Sahitya Akademi's Bi-Monthly Journal No. 210, July-Aug. 2002, Vol. XLVI No. 4, New Delhi. *Beast*, Chitra Mudgal, p. 20)

It is interesting to note the manner in which the writer takes the reader into the conflicting mental thought processes of the tongawalla in order to swell the juxtapositions of life and its demands in his mind are two opposition angles of the nights. The tongawalla is lost in his stream of consciousness and while these questions rush through his mind, he tugs resignedly at Sarwari's reins, who, hearing her masters loving voice, makes a clumsy forward movement. Observing her helplessness his previous sense of (despair) resilience persists; supposing Sarwari collapses in the middle of the road with the weight of the passengers "and the customers rolled off and fell down" (21), what would he do? This gloomy dread and hopelessness of the situation hangs constantly upon his sensibility (consciousness) until the Tonga is somehow pulled up to the bridge, with exertion. Hoping that Sarwari would be able to pull along just a little bit further. All this time, while the tonga has somehow proceeded forward, the mind of the tongawalla has travelled between (into) the past and becomes despondent over at the thought of his shrewish wife Linberda and her lacerating tongue, who according to him 'stems the enmity...against him and Sarwari' (21).

At this point, the writer tells us how the horse had been sick for twenty...'twenty-five days' (22) and how he, Aslam would coax her to stand and how Sarwari would fold her knees and fall back after an hour or so. Closing her rheumy eyes" (22). Despite the fact that all kinds of medicines had been administered to her—all of them had failed and he had grown panicky when Jumman Hakim cautioned (advised) him—to hope for the best. However, Jumman miyan also advises him to visit a fakir at Jama Masjid who is reputed to have cured people of 'incurable diseases' by tying a "(rotire) black thread onto people" (22).

It is interesting to note how the writer has delved into the inner recesses of the human psyche in portraying to how people tend to resort to superstitious beliefs when they can find no other means of saving the lives of their dear ones. Be it a man (term used in a kinder sense) or an animal. So Aslam returns, notwithstanding the continuances to administer the herbal medicines given to him by Jumman miyan and gradually notices that the blisters on Sarwari's legs had begun to heal but at a painfully slow speed; when advised by his neighbour Karim, who tells him not to think of earning money; nonetheless, he ruefully comprehends that since there was no money in the house; what was he to do? desperately falls at his wife's feet begging her to give him her silver anklets which he then sold to the village goldsmith 'at half or one-third of their price,' yet sadly, the injections fail, Sarwari is diagnosed to suffer from glanders; the disease had progressed too much, and only a miracle could cure her. Aslam wretchedly gasps the situation: that Sarwari had not long to live: (however), between this realization and his conscious effort to do all that he could for Sarwari, he resignedly accepts that he could do no more beyond what was destined to occur. "Indigenous medicines did not seem now to work on animals either..." (22). With these reflections he makes a faint attempt to reassure and console himself by musing, "—did his forefathers ever had injections given to their horses"? (22). He further contemplates: supposing the worst happened, what would be the result? I quote:

> Zubeida would bark at him like a dog who's spied a thief. Her sharp tongue tore him apart 'Luckless lives! From

> where am I to get food to feed you twice a day.... Shall I cut myself into pieces and fill your bellies?'... He's out of his mind, keeps caressing that half dead whore.... Even our kitchen utensils have been sold.... She'll swallow us all up before dying.... She's not a mare any more but my rival...shy are you destroying all of us along with her? Throw her out! (Mudgal, 23)

This forms the crux as well as the irony of the entire events that follow. While these words boomerang he remembers having struck his wife in the morning ordering her to shut her "foul mouth" and damning her "blasted tongue" saying: "The day this rival of your collapses we will all be compelled to swallow poison and finish ourselves off...." (23)

The writer here, with a few strokes of her pen, aptly conveys the message about the poor living conditions of the have-nots of society. She portrays Aslam's mental anguish over the dread of losing his house on one hand, and on the other, the burden of feeding his large family. Zubeida's distress (anguish) is no less. She is embittered because she is aware that there are no future prospects of feeding her family—if all the little they have is thrown away on a half-dead animal. Her misery is revealed in her suffering when she demands that her husband till her whether she should put 'live coals' in the mouths of the eight hungry mouths. Her protest as a mother and a human being is not only genuine but also justified. Aslam; conscious of these conditioned bearings could do nothing but once again strike his wife who challenges him with an ultimatum—that he look after his "Whelps" himself. The male ego is wounded to the core and once again he strikes her: Toad! Taad! The stinging force of his blows that felled the sobbing Zubeida to the ground (23).

The reader is made conscious (aware) of the situation with simple colloquial words and the impact it creates, is that of pity. It forces him (the reader) to react and reconsider the plight of the poor and the downtrodden in a very forceful manner. While all these incidents make Aslam recede into the past, he melancholy compares his own tired body to that of Sarwari's and finds consolation by thinking about his father who had migrated to Delhi to make a living, while he,—Aslam, was still a child who played gulli-danda, even so (however) he is rudely awakened from his revive by one of the passengers who chide him for having been driven half a mile beyond their destination. Wrapped up and lost in contemplation, Aslam returns to the temporal world, lovingly strokes Sarwari's flanks and notices the ordeal into which he has placed her;—her damp eyes tell a tale—"He thanks God for a clear sky, grabs the ten rupee note...the way a starving man grabs at a piece of bread" (24). Sarwari had saved him and his family from pangs of hunger that day.

The writer here lifts the veil from the face of reality against the grating consciousness of the tongawalla who is run between the thoughts of sustaining a hungry family, and the plight of the suffering arrival. A concrete picture of Aslam is dexterously drawn and reveals how the poor man is caught between Scylla and Charybdis. Who does he save? His suffering Sarwari—an irrational animal who can never complain—or his shrewish wife and children. As a caretaker of the family where does his duty lie? Aslam, the caretaker chooses to save his family and himself not only from the gruesome wrath but also from starvation. Aslam contemplates upon buying a kilo of biryani that would provide the hungry children with a feast since they had not seen meat for a week. But as soon as this idea is conceived it vanishes just as quickly; as the thoughts of Zubeida fill him with sorrow. And so rejecting the idea of buying biryani for the children, thinks it to be his duty to place the ten bucks in her palms saying: I quote:

> Here take your rival's earnings...
> She does not have the strength to
> Walk four steps yet she's managed to
> Carry nine passengers for you... (24)

Aslam is after all a human being. His heart seems to soften towards Zubeida as he is forced to fathom her basic goodness as a human being. When Aslam's first wife had abandoned him it was Zubeida who had looked after his five children along with her own three; although she had treated them with a difference—Aslam, notwithstanding, acknowledges that she did look after them all.

Having no further wish to carry any more passengers, he fondly caresses Sarwari while resting a while. The writer records this action filled with tenderness in the following manner. I quote:

> He took her face between his hands
> and gazed pityingly into her eyes. And
> saw a last burst of light
> flare up in those rheumy
> Saxena's words flashed through his
> mind, beating at him like a hammer
> "Consider yourself lucky if she lasts for one or two days..." (25)

Here the writer has very touchingly established a permanent bond between the master Aslam and the 'slave' Sarwari and while he still recalls the doctor's warning, a voice hails him once again. While he rejects the pleas of the first three groups of people, and

> Are you a man or a monster? If
> you cannot have sympathy for a
> dying beast and try to earn five or
> ten bucks more carrying a couple of
> fares, will you be set for life? Have
> patience. Be satisfied with what you've
> earned for the day. How long you
> and Sarwari have been together!
> She has always been satisfied—whether
> you gave her the best of fodder or the
> poorest. (25)

Here, the differences have been sharply contrasted between man, the selfish soul animal and Sarwari,—the beast who has always been satisfied with whatever was given to her for survival. The acceptance of her fate is meekly borne by Sarwari—but not by Aslam. Greed and temptation entice him, and although he is sensitive to the fact that Sarwari needs rest and that they must return home, because he has not failed to notice that she was giving strange looks and that "Her eyes were swimming in a pool of water. But, the revenue is once again broken by a lone passenger who wishes to ride up to Happy School. He wonders whether he should take her. Consoling himself that it was on his way home, he allows her to mount the tonga fixing the fare, for three rupees. He reins up at Happy School and with consternation glances at Sarwari's face. He is filled with dismay and misgivings as he observes her drooping eyes and quivering jaws which did not bode well" (26). She shivered and trembled depleted of strength, as if she had a fever. Now anguish is writ large upon his face as he realizes that her condition had deteriorated within that hour. Suddenly he experiences a sense of shame at the thought that he had exploited her. I quote:

> Not only does the beast understand
> his need but is cooperating with
> him continuously. And as for him,
> knowingly his exploiting her agony. (26)

All the while Aslam has been perfectly aware of Sarwari's tender condition and yet has overlooked its seriousness. The man's brute sense has made him numb towards Sarwari's silent acceptance of her fate and now she had used up "all her strength to remain on her feet". Aslam has been clearly forewarned that she "could collapse on the road any moment. It would be hard for her to pass the night.... What would he do without Sarwari!..."?

Lost in contemplation, the future now seems bleak. Once again cut off from the temporal world for a while, he wonders what he would do without Sarwari and that even though he would sell his "rickety tonga" it would not fetch him enough money. I quote:

> [His heart was overflowing. A flame of fire leapt up in his belly. His brain boiled over to pound at his temples....] The future seemed too awful to contemplate! and then Eight children – buzzing like wasps! Zubeida's poisonous tongue leaping out at him like a viper. Black venomous. How would he face all that? (26)

The situation is now tense. Aslam is terrified. The thought of feeding eight children now 'stings' his conscience. He compares them to wasps and Zubeida's tongue is metaphorically referred to as 'poisonous'. These gushing thoughts wound his psyche and while he still remains lost in these meditative reflections, a young girl driving a white Fiat rushes swiftly towards the Kotwali constantly blowing the horn—as if urging a warning of the impending calamity which was probably preordained—A bus comes up from the left side of the Fiat—Crowding the way. The girl makes a failing attempt to avoid the tonga that has unconsciously driven towards the middle of the road, and the right mudguard edge bangs into Sarwari's left leg so that she instantaneously collapses in a heap and life immediately comes to a standstill. I quote:

> The vehicles on both sides come to a halt, ...and an ear-splitting cacophony of horns rose around them. The ones in front san Sarwari collapse in a heap.... Her injured frame jerked violently and her quivering jaws foamed. Her eyes grew fixed and a thin stream of blood, flowed from her left leg, which kept shuddering along with her body. (26)

The writer here has built up a tense situation in which she has focused the reader's attention on the actions and reactions of man at large, apart from touching upon the mob psychology; which gives the story an edge and while the animal his half-dead, the terrified girl Sheena, watches the steadily growing crowd turn against her. Taking advantage of the situation, the tongawalla wails beating his breast, and collapsing on Sarwari's bloodstained body curses "Oh God! Oh God! I'm ruined; totally ruined!... She's killed...my Sarwari...taken away my livelihood! ...I had paid a full eight thousand for her..." (27).

The girl's mother offers him a hundred to a hundred fifty rupees as compensation the matter remains unsettled. The hue and cry increases and ultimately the matter is taken to the police station, where a case is registered. However, the tongawalla is denied justice and the tables are turned upon him. He is harshly scolded, and pressurized to take back the charge. After several unfruitful attempts the girl's influential father Mr. Tewari is summoned at the behest of the Station House Officer, Gehlot. Havaldar Bishan Singh, now waxes him to take two thousand rupees in order to avoid trips to the court that might prove disastrous for him. Reluctantly Aslam demands five thousand. He is badly beaten up until meekly exclaims "What can a blind man ask for except two eyes!" (31) in short. The brutal beating, had had its effect. Aslam is given two thousand rupees and the matter is dismissed.

Sheena, the young girl has all this while been a silent observer. Who, "looked like a prisoner...first released from jail". She drops her gaze, and with this sentence, the writer conveys the mental agony suffered by her during this ordeal. Nonetheless, the story does not end here. This anti-climax finally leads to an ironical climax and denouncement when, the story takes a critical turn in the life of Aslam whose agony over the death of Sarwari wakes him up suddenly in the middle of the night. He is tired and fagged out, mentally as well as physically, when he is startled by the "sharp sound of a mare whining". He cries "Its Sarwari's voice—that musical, rhythmic whinny!" (34). The vision of Sarwari is so deeply stamped in his consciousness that he hurriedly gets up, opens the door expecting to behold his beloved Sarwari, but all that he is met with outside is "the deep silence of the night.... And...the lonesome looking tonga, bereft of Sarwari's presence.... Where is Sarwari...? (34). The reflection now comes to surface and the writer focuses her attention on the spiritual...of a guilty man. I quote:

> How can she be here? He had left her a lifeless corpse on the road; for the municipal van which came to collect the abandoned bodies. How fast he had sped from the scene. (34)

Swiftly he enters the room. Wildly searches for 'something beneath his pillows'. Finds what he was searching for, presses it to his heart and; I quote:

> Unable to suppress the rising tide of emotion that was bursting out of his chest, he howled as loud as a tree that has been severed from its root and came crashing to ground, sending the piteous sound of its destruction to all the corners of the earth. (34) (He is filled with remorse)

All the pent up feelings over the loss of Sarwari now burst upon him like a river in flood. He sobs so violently that Zubeida, confounded by her husband's strange behaviour rushes towards him, in a vain attempt to console him saying that sooner or later Sarwari would have died anyway and it is now that the writer gives the story a twist in order to expose the guilty conscience of the tongawalla who confesses. I quote:

> No...she did not leave us on her own.... I killed her before she could.... I cashed on her death! Deliberately ran her into the car...with the thought that she was going to die in

> any case. If she collided with the car she would earn her own price in her death...these notes are not money, they are Sarwari's flesh and blood! (34)

The truth was out at last. Zubeida's heart twisted. The hand, "which was massaging Aslam's back, stopped on its own" (34). Zubeida's heart is wrenched. She who called Sarwari, a whore and her rival is dumb struck, while Aslam, the actual beast remains wretchedly conscious of having killed her. The temptation of material gain had blinded him so much that he had lost control over his humaneness. The tongawalla Aslam is now shown to be an entirely new character from that of a murderer of moral values. The question that remains to be answered is, who is the beast? The irrational Sarwari who surrenders her life or the rational human being, Aslam, the tongawalla?

Deepa Agarwal, the translator of the story has poignantly captured the true essence of the story in English. She has aptly revealed with subtle irony, the end of the story, through the character of the protagonist. The story is bathed in realism. It is a true picture of the downtrodden who struggle to earn their livelihood and live in pitiable conditions. The writer also projects a very realistic picture of those who are in power and carry its weight upon their shoulder—Power, prestige and money rule their lives. Muscle power draws action in the garb of performing duties; Mr. Tiwari represents materialism—with which he buys his daughter's freedom. Hand and glove with him are men of justice who represent the State authority.

Deepa Agarwal's translation has wielded her style so powerfully in exposing the character of Aslam that the reader is inadvertently drawn towards the tongawalla sufferings and his anguish besides human relationship. The plight of his tormented heart is effectively conveyed, and the entire story is written in the stream of consciousness technique as experimented and perfected by James Joyce and Virginia Woolf of the Western World. Just as Woolf's Clauisson Dalloway and Septinous Warren Smith return to the conscious and temporal world with the striking of the Big Ben, so also Aslam, the tongawalla is always returned to the present world by a call for the tonga, by the passengers who hail him. This breaks the thought process of the tongawalla who take the reader back and forth in time, and breaks the monotony of the serious musings of the protagonist—Aslam. The end has a sting—but one which is pathetic.

To conclude, I would like to state that English translations of stories composed in regional or Indian languages, are excellently well written. Besides retaining 'original flavour' translators have become 'a source of strength' for the leading community. Translated works are acceptable to readers because in this way they are able to understand and relate themselves to all literatures of the world which thereby helps them to establish a silent bond not only with the writer, but also with the social and cultural traditions of the place in country in which the story is set. A demand is steadily rising across the world for such standard translations so that even may reach out to one another. A global world demands global literature and the time seems not far off when probably each one of us would ourselves be writing a translation of our own favourite stories.

15

SADDALE (SILENCE)

MANJUNATHA BEVINAKATTI

When the Goravappa exhorts the oracle crouching on long bow at the time of the fair he warns the public to maintain silence and for that he uses the word "Saddale". This proclamation is called "Karanika" or oracle and it forms the most important part of the fair. This foretells the prospects of the succeeding year with regard to seasonal rain, crop, people and the world. The believers of Mylaralinga believe in their ups and downs during the next year with utmost faith interpreting this oracle. The soothsayer perching on the high bow, shakes his head and after warning the public announces the oracle. Immediately the thousands of people gathered at the site maintain pin drop silence. Soon after the goravappa lifts his head above, looks at the sky and pronounces few words which are considered as karnika or oracle. The people believe those words as those that have come from the mouth of Shiva.

Mylaralinga's tradition, densely spread over Karnataka, Andhra Pradesh, Maharashtra and Goa, is of special significance. It is a complex tradition devoid of caste, community and class. It is an uphill task to conjoin and state such a complex and rich tradition under a single definition. The present theoretical pressure is about unified India. There is an adamant attempt to bring under a single authority all the different voices, sections and the separated cultural groups. In history conciliation of all religions and bringing amity among all the groups has been continuously taken up as a constructive work. This effort was made on the firm foundation of strong religious belief, but this was not as decisive and serious as the one that was carried out in the 20th century. Yet it has noiselessly subdued the other religious traditions.

Consideration of cultural unity and religious unity as one and the same is only a mirage. This is a cunning attempt to negate everything and to oppress the different voices. The study of Mylaralinga's cultural tradition has to be taken up in this framework and if undertaken in a different route it may lead to separate dimensions.

Majority of the shepherd or kuruba community has adopted Mylara as their divine god of worship. The epic of the lengthy poetry of Mylara embedded in the lives of the worshippers abounds in curiosity. This lengthy poetry of Mylara Linga is one among the best fold epics of Karnataka and it describes the destruction of the villainous Mylara demon, protecting the righteous people, marriages, mysteries and attempts to draw the attention of devotees towards God etc.

Many incidents in the epic are mostly symbolic and are of inquisitive nature. In order to understand the tradition or the path of Mylara Linga it is necessary to know the cultural background of India as a whole. In its thousands of years of history, India has been the birth place of many races, cultures and religious groups. It has also paved the way for conflicts and downfalls and has accepted the new system that emerged as a result of such conflicts and downfalls. As and when these paths became worn out new ones were created and followed. In this way India has become a land of complex cultural activities.

Mylaralinga's tradition is an important part of this culture. The original inhabitants of this region and the Aryans who migrated here had both conflicts and co-operation among them and it resulted in a new culture. Keeping this background in view it is necessary to study Karnataka of middle ages and about the sect of Mylara Linga's with utmost intensity and eagerness.

It was Veerabhadra who put an end to the practice of yajna of the Aryans. Veerabhadra, a shaivite, encouraged the priesthood and attained the rank of a god of worship. Mylara Linga was originally a leader of Shaiva group. This Mylaralinga tradition continued to flourish as an alternative to the other Shaiva sects of Kapalika, Kalamukha, Lakkulesha and such other mystic groups.

Mylara's story is an example of Shaivite story process. Formerly classical literature and poetry had to conform to the rules and limitations prescribed in Sanskrit books. The Shaiva intellectuals for the first time walked out of these limitations and turned their attention towards new paths. Devotional poets like Harihara concentrated their thoughts about the narrator, devotee and god. The epic of Mylara gets importance here. Apart from the three persons involved as stated above another object gains importance as the fourth one and that is this materialistic world. This last object unfolds itself as an intensive motive force in the story. Tree, forest, nature and biological changes are not very important according to Harihara, all these are pushed aside in his stream of devotion.

The forest is the prime part of the shepherds, life as described in the beginning of the epic. There is no life for the shepherds without the forest. Forest, caste, nature, animals etc., which are inseparable parts of life are interlocked in the life of Mylara. Dualism which overcomes idealism is exposed here as truth. Mylara and his tradition appear here as un-jointed paths. The story conveys dualities but at the end it solidifies and presents itself as a curious cultural symbol.

According to history the shepherds are considered as a migrated tribe. When this nomadic tribe established itself in one place, Mylara Linga became a cultural hero. Later on Mylara Linga faced the atrocities of the already established races of Brahmins and Veerashaivas who were in large numbers. For this oppressive fight he united all the lower caste people of the North Karnataka and achieved glory.

Lets us turn our attention to the holy places of Mylara Linga and the various names by which he is hailed. Let us study his history and the details of inscriptions about him. We shall also study his relationships with mystic groups, his utterances among the folk proverbs, in the poetry, stories, local histories, practices, fairs, writings, literature etc. From all these sources we learn the fact that Mylara Linga originally came from a shepherd race who led a nomadic life to care for the sheep. As a result of cultural evolution they settled down at some places. They also took to farming along with shepherding. They had to face the wrath of the other tribes who had settled down there before them. Mylara Linga must have resisted the onslaught of the other tribes and given protection to his followers. So he became a local god to them. Slowly he attained the steps of glory. The influence of the "Shakta" school of thought might have assisted him. Perhaps this must have influenced his wife, Malachi who attained the status of "Shakta goddess". Her followers might have taken Mylara in their folds and raised him to higher plane. After embracing "Shakta fold" he might have become an incarnation of Bhairavi. In consonance with this new elevation his vehicle etc. might have been created. His tradition is noticed in Karnataka, Maharashtra and a few parts of Andhra Pradesh.

While among a class of people the influence of Mylara was on the increase people of other religious groups raised their fingers against him and decried him. Gradually mal-propaganda against him subsided and he was accepted as a divine being from the devotees of Shiva. When we observe the large number of his followers today we know about his folk popularity.

The 'Goravas', the staunch devotees of Mylara, today recite the epic of Mylara Linga. The experts are of the opinion that 'Guru' is the root word from which 'Gorava' is derived. In Kittel's dictionary the meaning is given as beggars in the name of Shiva. In North Karnataka they are called by the names of Gwarappa, Vaggayya, Vaagya and so on and in South Karnataka they are called Gorava, Goggayya and Gadabaddayya. There are differences only in dress and practices among these two groups. The Gorava of North Karnataka has a turban on his head, wears a long rough woollen coat with a few emblems on it and carried a trident and a drum (damaru) in his hands. A few bells will be hanging from his drum. Round his neck is tied a tiger skin bag holding holy turmeric. On the forehead he smears turmeric paste and holds a cane in the hand. There is a rough woollen shawl on his arm and on it long steel chains will be dangling up to his knee. The Gorava of South Karnataka carries a bell, tiger skin and steel bands around his arms. There is a necklace of cowries round the neck and a shield of cowries across his chest. The shield is surrounded by strings of cowries. A small trident, a cane, a flute and drum are his other adornments. Round the waist he wears a belt of tiger skin and as footwear he puts on wooden slippers made of berry thorns. His headdress is a hat made from the hair of bear or sometimes simply a hat of coiled hair. The forehead and the exterior of the eyelids will be covered with 'Vibhuti' or holy ash. There will be a thick paste of vermilion all along the forehead. The face presents a fearsome appearance of red and white colours. There are also female goravas.

As among 'the devaraguddas' these goravas also receive 'diksha' or holy order from the seniors. This procedure is called 'mane kattu'. Usually the eldest son in the family is ordained as a gorava. For conferring the 'diksha' a woollen carpet is spread and the borders are fixed. In the middle a Kalasa and mirror are placed. The feet of the gorava are covered with shining metallic powder and a yellow thread called 'Kankana' is tied round his right wrist. A necklace of cowries is tied round the neck. For ordaining him to the gorava order the presence of dasayya, jogayya and jangamayya is a must. A pearl is tied round his neck. Then he must take a pledge in the name of the god of his worship. He must swear that he will not speak ill of his parents, jogis and jangamas. If a stray cattle is grazing in a field he shall not drive it away. If a calf is sucking the udder he shall not detach it from its mother. He will not wear any footwear. He will not travel in a cart or kill a serpent. Such a gorava is called Mylara Linga's "Gudda". From that day he can go to any place of any region to beg. The devotees obtain "Bhandara" or sacred turmeric from him and pay some money to him when he visits their houses.

The study of fold epic started from the Romantic age or middle ages. The fold epics were utilized to exhibit patriotism, to unite the communities and to proclaim their traditional grandeur.

The Goravas sing the epic during fairs and boat service. Before beginning they offer coconut to the deity and at conclusion, the coconut is broken and offered to god. Then its pieces are given to devotees. Formerly at the end of each chapter a coconut was split and offered. But that practice is now dispensed with. The Goravas dramatize the epic to create interest to the listeners. We can notice the effect of the song, dance and drama when it is recited. The epic is not accepted simply as a bye-product but is considered as a process. They do not merely recite the epic as it is but also enhance its beauty by explaining the incidents with their creative originality.

The age old tradition is followed with a little change here and there. It accepts the reality in the background of social philosophy. It is worth discussing about the way the epic is presented and dramatized. This powerful dramatization is perceived as non-Brahmanical tradition. The social reformers and educators use this dramatic method to convey their ideas. The accessories needed for this method are the geographical and cultural environment around us. For this story process the psychology of the individuals that gather to listen is studied. The path of idolatry is considered more effective than philosophical social tradition. The understanding of materialistic relationship is more helpful than seeking liberation from worldly affairs. The philosopher here finds the individuality of the poet exceeding the limits of speech, dramatics and acoustics. The poet or the story-teller pulls down the sublime and latent ideas to the silly and worldly process. This is the greatness of devotional poetry. These devotional poets with their manual efforts and daily occurrences try to explain the social realities that confront life. The prosaic writers (Vachanakararu) hailing from lower castes have done this work with devotion. The essence of these indigenous epics lies in the discussion type of story-telling. Instead of solo narration the discussion type is more effective and impressive. As an alternative to disinteresting formal narration this indigenous presentation has overrun the Vedic tradition.

When this epic is examined with a critical view we identify some new features. The artists who sing this epic have made use of more than 150 types of 'laya', 'Sollu' and 'raagas-taalas'. The melancholic (Karunaa Rasa) emotional tunes adopted here are appropriate. "Khamacha" and "Bheemplas" raagas are prominent here. Among the taalas 'Kerava' and 'daadara' are outstanding and the "Bhajan" tekas are also used. These songs are sung to the note of black 3 and 5.

Example – 1:

Raaga : Khamach **Tala : Kerava.**

Mangalenniri	Devage$_{ssss}$		
Sa Sa Ri Sa Sa	Ga Ga Ma Ga Ri Sa		
Sriya	Meenagundi	Mallayyage	
Pa Pa	Ma Ga Ri Sani	Sa Ri Sa Sa Sa ‖1‖	
Mallaiahage	Belaguve	Naaruti	Aadarinda
Pa Pa Pa	Da Pa Ma Ma	Ma Pa Ma	Sa Ma Ga Ga
Aettiroo	Idana$_s$	Mudadinda	
Ga Ga Ga	Ma Ga Ri$_S$	Sa Ni Sa Ri Sa	
Malammage	Belaguve	Naaruti	Hastadinda
Pa Pa Pa	Da Pa Ma Ma	Ma Pa Ma	Sa Ma Ga Ga
Nanu	Ninage$_s$	Belaguvenu	
Ga Ga Ga	Ma Ga Ri Sa	Ni Sa Ri Sa Sa	
Andu	Kumarage	Indu	Mallaiage
Pa Pa Pa	Da Pa Ma Ma	Ma Ma Ma	Pa Ma Ga Ga
Melgiri	Vasaga	Madevage	
Ga Ga Ga	Ma Ga Ri Sa	Ni Sa Ri Sa Sa	

Example – 2:

Raaga : Khamach **Tala : Daadara.**

Taayini	Nenadeva	Tandeena		Nenedeva
Ga Ga Ga	Ga Ga Ga	Ri$_s$ Ri Ga		Ri$_s$ Sa Sa Sa
Tande	Mallaiahana	Padavoo		
Ga Ga	Ga Ga Ga Ri	Ri$_s$ Ga Pa		
Tande	Mallaiahana	Padava	Hididare	
Sa Sa	Ma$_s$ Ma Ma	Ma Ma Ma	Ma Ma Ma Pa	
Kelida	Varagala	Needuvanu		
Pa Da Da	Pa Ma Pa	Ga Ga Ma Ri Sa		
Kelida	Varagala	Needuva	Devarige	Saranede
Sa Ri Ri Sa	Sa Ri Ri Sa	Sa Ri Sa	Sa Ri Ri Ga	Ni Sa Sa Ri
Naavu	Saranendevoo			
Ga Ga	Ri Sa Sa Sa$_s$			
Saranendevoo	Naavi	Saranendevoo		
Ga Ga Ga Ri Ri Ri	Ri Ri	Ni Ni Ni Sa Ri Ga Ri Sa Sa		

Example – 3:

Raaga : Bheemplas **Tala : Kerava.**

Gange	Malavva	Ninna	
Sa Sa	Pa Da Da	Pa Pa	
Gandana	Valivudu		
Ma Ma Sa	Ma Ga Ri Sa		
Bandaara	Cheela	Balagaile	
Sa Ri Ri	Saa Ni	Pa Ga Ma Sa	
Baa	Nanna	Maa	Guruve
Pa	Ma Ma	Ga Ga Ri Sa	

Example – 4:

Raaga : Bheemplas **Tala : Kerava.**

Sobana	Aennire	
Sa Sa Sa	Pa Pa Pa	
Sobana	Annire	
Sa Da Ni Da	Pa Pa Pa	
Sobanavenni	Shivaganni	Sobannave
Ma Pa Pa Ma Ga Ri	Ri Sa Ri Ga	Ga Ga Ri Sa

Example – 5:

Raaga : Bheemplas(Mishra) **Tala : Kaavali.**

Shiva	Kondakara	Kodanu	Rara	Ma
Sa Sa	Ri Ma Ma	Ma Ri Ri	Ga Ri	Sa Ni
Mallaiahna	Kondaka	Swami	Namisu	
Ni Ni Sa Sa	Ri Ga Ga Ri	Ri Ma	Ma Ma Ma	
Taanu	Rara	M_{ss} ||Pallavi||		
Ma Ma	Ga Ri	Sa Ni Sa		

The taala and laya employed here are mainly manipulated in double qualities (*Duguna*). This is the main nature of folklore laya and daati. The taalas, 'Kerava', 'Daadara' and Bhajan 'tekas' are specially intended for dance patterns for presenting melancholy tunes. In addition to these 'taalas', 'Khamacha' and 'Bheem Palas' raagas are quite necessary. More than half of the epic conveys the emotion of melancholy. In order to break the boredom of a single 'laya', the narration of the story includes lallaby (Jogula), Sobane (Wedding song), ballad (Lavani), drum beats, grinding and pounding styles of songs. These multi-directional methods assist in creating interest among the listeners. This reveals the creative abilities of singers.

While ending the lines and the stages of 'Laya' the singer makes use of vowels and consonants to the best advantage and this is a noteworthy technique. These additions, more than the literature of the song, help in completing the 'taalas' and 'Layas'. The additions that are employed are 'ni', 'ba', 'aa', 'e', 'eega' and 'aaga'.

Example:

Sugar added milk
To god offered
Relishingly eaten in the boat squatting
Come O' master, my master.

Datura |ni| ash
Wheat ash Mallayya
The paper ash scattered
'O' god of gods.

This poetry is fervently studied with the sole purpose of identifying how the folk music forms the base of elite music. In other words the elite music is a revised form of folk music. There is a belief that the folk music does not conform to taala, laya or raaga, but on scrutiny we can say that this belief is erroneous. We can recognise these three qualities when the epic is sung. The story taker has displayed his creative capacity by singing the songs in a variety of taalas, layas and raagas. The established elite music conforms to single 'laya' but the fold music has the freedom to render the song in its own style. The singer adopts the common method while singing the epic. He also tries to retain its various dimensions. This fact is made clear from the unity of layas, repetition of song, its onward movement and other intricacies. During recitation the oracles of Mylara Linga are exhorted heroically at intervals. They dance emotionally while singing and inflict their bodies with sharp thick needles to give a religious touch to the demonstration. This fearsome exhibition leads us to consider Mylara Linga's epic on a different ground.

On a study of the epic of Mylara Linga we notice that the incidents described in the story are linked to the practices that are followed today during fairs and congregations. The epic is not mere poetry but it is a part of fairs and procedures wherein the incidents are reproduced. In it the age old history is repeated. Mylara Linga married Komali, a tribal lady; influenced a lady of a noble family of Ranibennur to become his devotee; gave his woollen coat to dhobi to wash it and converted him to become his follower and such incidents helped him to propagate his cult.

In the poetry we come across the super human power of Mylara Linga and attempts made to deify him. The poetry is complicated and at the end we are made to believe that he is an incarnation of god. All this looks like a puppet show and the puppets appear to be controlled by a divine power.

The poetry leaves an indelible impression about the exemplary nature of man's dynamic force and spiritual heroism.

REFERENCES

Kannada Series

Bevinakatti, Manjunatha. 1999. *Mailaralingana Kavya.* Hampi: Vidyaranya Prasaranga, Kannada University.

Kulkarni, B.S. 1964. "Mailar–Karnatakada Devaru, Maharastrada Kuladevaru Andarenu?". *Journal of the Karnataka University Humanities* (Vol. VIII).

——. 1965. "Mallari-Martanda-Bhirava Ondu Daivatavoo Athava Samukta Daivatavoo". *Journal of the Karnataka.*

Neginahala, M.B. 1992. *Mailarlinga Khandoba.* Dharwada: Prasaranga, Karnataka University.

English Series

1984. "Dasara at Devaragudda, Ritual and play in the cult of Mailara/ Khandoba". *South Asian Digest of Regional Writing,* 10.

1984. "The Mallari-Khandoba Myth as Reflected in Folk Art and Ritual", Anthropos. 79.

1993. *Pastoral Deities in Western India.* Delhi: Oxford University Press.

1994. *Mylarlinga Tradition: Performance Study.* Udupi: Regional Resources Centre for Folk Performing Artists.

16

The Short Stories of Manoj Das: A Humanistic Approach

ALIYA SHOBI

Manoj Das, a renowned name in the realm of Indo-Anglican literature has authored some 12 volumes of short-stories, two novels, 13 collection of Children's Literature in English, so far. Born in Orissa, he is bi-lingual in his writings and he writes with the same ease and comfort in English as in his mother-tongue, Oriya.

Humanism is a branch of philosophy that lays stress on human life, human beings and human-relationship at the centre of the universe. The Humanists are concerned with everything human in this world and they attach supreme importance to human values. The origin of the term "Humanism" dates back to the ancient Greco-Roman culture which amply used the concept to explore human relationship in its varied forms and facets. The 15th century Renaissance scholars renamed 'Humanism' as 'Medieval Scholasticism'. Alexander Pope, the prominent master of Neo-Classicism in the English Literature writes, "The proper study of mankind is man".[1] The very definition has a clear-cut blending of Humanism which stresses "man in relation to mankind". Similarly, when we go through the oriental epics like *The Ramayana, The Mahabharatha, The Gita* etc., we find the exploration of moral and ethical values in man in relation to the universe.

The chief tenets of Humanism can be noted as follows:

1. Humanism glorifies the existence of man on the earth.

2. It says that the basic nature of human beings is good.
3. Man can realise his destiny only by developing his human potentialities.
4. Solving human problems with the help of reason is more important than religious beliefs.[2]

When we analyse the stories of Manoj Das in connection with aforesaid traits of Humanism we will see that maximum of them present a clear-cut blending of the doctrine. First of all, the characters in his stories, either engaged in silly or petty plotting or in solemn and magnanimous activities, are all given a human touch by the writer. The writer, in fact, does not see anything called 'villainous' in his characters. He rather glorifies them with their moral and immoral pursuits. This notion in the writer springs up from his deep vision and profound understanding of human life. He visualizes all human beings as gifts by the Almighty to the mother earth and hence they cannot be bad. This is in fact a superb act of glorification of man by the writer. Some examples from different stories may be mentioned in this connection.

In the story *The Different Man*, Pratap Singh tries to reform the character of others in his surroundings, but he fails to judge the mood and the psychological aspect of the man he is going to reform and hence he becomes a subject of derision. He asks the young 'trio' buying cigarettes:

> When did you take to smoking ? Why did you pledge your health to the vampire of tobacco ?... You consider yourselves very clever. Don't you?... Don't you know the carton announcing "Cigarette smoking is injurious to health"?... The trio counter-attack in a spasm of anger with their question to him, "Why did you get married when the ancient 'Rishis' had pronounced warning against sex...?"[3]

In the above delineation what Pratap Singh lacks is the note of euphemism in his tone. Reformation is welcome but one needs to see whether the man one is going to reform is mentally prepared and logically and situationally agreeable to listen to one's views. A reformist needs to be a psychologist capable enough to study the time, place and person before sermonizing.

In the story *The Murderer* we have a portrait of the

villainous Zamindar of the village whom Vinu is supposed to have murdered. But at the end of the story we find the landlord has atoned for his sin by leading the life of a mendicant. Vinu has also shown a superb example of servility and honesty till the end. Is it not the glorification of human life by the writer with his indirect indictment that nobody in the world is a devil and a derailed man can set himself back to the tract of nobility by adopting asceticism ?

As Maxim Gorkey has said, "Man is a god in himself". In the stories of Manoj Das the idea is reflected to the fullest extent giving no room to negativism and scepticism.

In the story *The Crocodile's Lady*, the writer portrays the great love and enthusiastic longing of a foreigner towards 'Indian Mysticism'. India, a land of naked *fakirs*, snake-charmers, itinerant mendicants and people with Bohemian existence may not be having a place on the map for its great scientific and technological advancement but one thing the rest of the world is sure of is that life throbs and thrills in India for its mystery. An Australian writer, Jac Hansen, observes, "God lives in India..."[4] and truly the Indians live with the notion that whatever they do, wherever they go and whatever situation they confront with, they overcome as they love God. Manoj Das finds this aspect of the Indian character figure out in his stories. The Crocodile's Lady, despite her mysterious disappearance for a decade, is sympathesized, honoured, loved and revered by the people.

In the story *The Mountain*, Manoj Das reflects the beauty of Nature to be the eternal abode of solace and peace for mankind. Sagar Babu, the one time hunter is fascinated by the charm of the mountain and leads the life of a mendicant denouncing worldly pleasure. 'Nature throbs with life—a life with a divine existence' a life that attracts the world of human beings to its lap. It is for this reason that the experimenters of the eternal values of life take to a forest, living in a calm solitude. The trees, the birds, the beasts and the brooks—all sing the glory of creation. Manoj Das paints an anthropomorphized Nature in the story *The Mountain*.

Humanism figures man—the creator of his problems and man—the finder of solution to it with his reason. In the stories

The Murderer, The Mystery of the Missing Cap and *The Irrational,* we find the characters which have matured themselves by finding out solutions with the proper justification in their life. The landlord in *The Murderer* takes to a renounced living, the ministers in *The Mystery of the Missing Cap* and *The Irrational* give up politics as they realize their nefarious nexus with selfish pursuits in it. The story-teller says in the background "power lurks below the surface of your consciousness, renounce it and you will live the life of a man".

Humanism finds a clear interpretation in the story *Farewell to a Ghost* by Manoj Das who places an Anthropomorphic presentation of a ghost in it. The villagers believe in the presence of a ghost which has been treated as a member among them. They offer her food and invite her to the festivals and rituals and even solicit her auspicious presence in the day-to-day events and incidents. The ghost is no less than the headman of the village.

Manoj Das is a humourist of a special cadre. Even if the reformist in him satirizes the existing dogmas and superstitions in the Indian society, he is never purgent and fierce in his approach. His satire and humour are tinged with his love for the mankind. His characters love the humanity with their tears and laughters and hence give a message that life should be accepted with a smile with its follies and fallacies. There are stories like *The Man of Wart and other Stories, The Naked, The General, Mystery of the Missing Cap, The Princess, The Marital Expedition* and the like where humour finds a gentle, smiling, soothing and human touch. In *The Man of Wart and other Stories,* the wart on the temple of a man has been the object of mockery and humour. Instead of undergoing a surgical operation to get rid of the cancerous growth of the wart, the man moves for a record in the Guinness Book for having the largest wart in the world. Similarly, Bhanu Singh in the story, *The Naked* cannot make up his mind as to how to welcome a group of nudists. "Would it be fair to welcome the nudists with clothes?" he observes. The General, who is supposed to have won in several battles with great display of chivalry finds himself defeated and diffident to pronounce his briefest dialogue, a hilarious military laughter on a stage-show and it leads to a mild fever and heart-attack. Likewise, in the story,

The Mystery of the Missing Cap, a monkey has been treated as the best admirer of political ideology of the minister.

But the readers of Manoj Das have to be aware of the fact that his humour never amounts to a vulgar or derogatory implication. They are always blended with a humanistic touch. We love to laugh at the characters because we really love them, is the message from the story-teller's pen. Another important aspect of the art of Manoj Das is his master-craftsmanship of presenting a lively description of abstracts and inanimate objects in his stories. The setting sun behind the mountain, the rising moon over the valley, the whistling of the gust of wind over the village in the midst of greenery have all their language to talk and to sing the glory of the creation of God. They all appear human in his stories. They are just like any Tom, Dick and Harry and are, in fact, an integral part and parcel of human society. A few examples illustrate this:

> But his eyes were filled with the tears of gratitude. Who but the sky and the ocean would understand what the naked deity had meant to him....

In the story *The Crocodile's Lady*, nature appears human:

> That a hundred cattle would march through fenceless paddy-fields with absolute abstinence obeying a 'tiny-tots' hooting, was as fantastic as the Pied Piper's magic. Wonderful was the hung rainbow, fantastic the revelation and ninety-seven per cent of our villagers lived quite contented without having seen a locomotive or a cinema....

Similarly, *The Owl* presents nature in the shape of a musician as in the lines:

> At Vishalpur the sunset seemed to follow a certain rhythm and the birds which flew back to their old trees on the marshland at the western end of the village, did so beating their wings in tune with it....

In the aforesaid quotes Nature has been humanized, glorified and even integrated to the very spirit of human life. Manoj Das is truly a master artist, a true humanist and a saintly character who perceives a close affinity between the human and the divine in his stories.

REFERENCES

1. Pope Alexander. 1982. *Essay on Man.* Anthology of Verses' Muses Bower, New Delhi: Orient Longman.
2. Wimsatt B. (Jr.) and Cleanth Brooke. 1957. *Literary Criticism.* New Delhi: OUP.
3. Manoj Das. 2001. *Selected Fiction.* New Delhi: Penguin.
4. Hansen Jac. 1994. *God Lives in India.* NSA (*SB Reviews,* Australia) 129.

17

The Spiritual Trauma of the Mother of a Naxalite Son

KIRAN SHUKLA

Hajar Chaurashir Ma written by Mahasweta Devi in Bengali in 1973 and translated by Samik Bandyopadhyay in English language as *'Mother of 1084'* is very sensitive and thought provoking novel. It is an insightful exploration of a complex relationship between the personal and political. It is the psychological, emotional and spiritual struggle and trauma of a mother whose beloved son dies in a Naxalite movement. One morning she awakes by the shattering news from telephone that her Naxalite son is lying dead in the police morgue.

In this novel, there is no historical account of the Naxalite movement. It is portrayed only in its urban phase during 1971-74.

In fact the Naxalite movement was the movement based on the Marxist theory but got the virulent form, *Karl Marx (1818-1883)* gave his views on scientific socialism in his great book *Das Kapital*. This was a powerful theoretical arm of proletariats in their class struggle against capitalistic slumber.

In Russia in 1917 there was movement during the era of *Lenin* and *Stalin* against the Jar. The society divided into two class. First of capitalists and second of farmers and labourers. So there was a big gap between the two. The conditions of the lower class became quite bad due to the rise of capitalism and so the dictatorship of proletariat was raised.

"The proletariat during its contest with the bourgeoisie is compelled by the force of circumstances, to organize itself as a class...by means of a revolution, it makes itself the ruling class, and as such sweeps away by force the old conditions of productions."[1]

According to *Karl Marx* "when the socialist society will be in its destination...only then can the narrow horizon of bourgeois right be fully left behind and society inscribe on its banner: from each according to his ability, to each according to his needs.

This was the ideology accepted by Lenin and Stalin in Russia. This revolution of proletariat came to China during the reign of *Mao-Tse-tung.* But all the ideologies were in its virulent form there. During the decades of 60s and 70s it started in Northern West Bengal in India. The movement started from the rural areas and spread to the urban areas. There were two parties C.P.I. (M-L) and C.P.I. (M). C.P.I. (M-L) followed this ideology in its virulent form. *Charu Majumdar* and *Kanu Ṣanyal* were its leaders. In this Naxalite movement there was integrity, selflessness. There was guts to die for a cause. Started with the ideologies the movement strayed from its path and became violent. There was military force and police retaliation against the C.P.I. (M-L) Urban guerrillas. There was no mercy for any C.P.I. (M-L) Cadre or supporter if caught. Certain localities and suburbs of Calcutta were affected by the Naxalite movement and the military force and police retaliation. Some brilliant students of the middle class who joined the party were taught the ideologies as if there was nothing else important for them. Rather they were brain washed of all the social values. They were taught that the freedom could not come from the path society and the state followed. It will come only through the barrel of the gun.

The concept of the story is based on the Naxalite movement and a mother's spiritual struggle when her Naxalite son is shot dead. The negligence of the hypocrate father towards his children and of the hypocrate husband towards his wife along with his dominant actions and attitudes leads the story to the culmination of spiritual struggle and to the turning point of Brati's life to total destruction. It is a spiritual and emotional dilemma of an apolitical mother who remains unaware of true Brati throughout his life. Her quest of the reasons of death of her martyred Naxalite son takes her closer to her dead son.

Sujata often dreams of the morning of 22 years ago when Brati was born. She remembers of the agony she had to bear. She had already had 3 children Jyoti, Neepa and Tuli. She had had to bear all the pain alone herself. No one was to care for her. Even her husband was careless. It was the early morning of seventeenth January 1948 when Brati was born. She remembers it 2 years before. It was again 17th January the telephone rang. She lifted the receiver in a half awakened daze. She had fainted after the news of her son's death. In Kantapukur in the police morgue there was again same anguish when she tries to identify her dead son. It was more painful for her that her husband did not care to identify his dead son. In spite of that he had had to pull so many strings to hush up the news that his son had died such a scandalous death. Even he did not allow Sujata to take his car. Otherwise anybody could identify the car. Thus Brati was wiped away by his own father.

Dibyannath's trying to suppress the news of his son's scandalous death shows disgust towards Brati. It is on the top when he and Jyoti, his elder son did not offer the dead Brati the lighted stick to set his body aflame on the funeral pyre. The writer exposes the morality of the family through the stream-of-consciousness of Sujata.

Sujata was subservient, silent, faithful and almost without an existence of her own. After Brati's death, she started to become conscious of her own importance, existence, alienation. she was dominated by her husband and mother-in-law. She had been quite meek. The affection, respect, and support which she should have got from the family, she lacked, that was the reason of her decision to stuck to her job. Though mother-in-law and husband went on complaining that she wanted to be independent that she did not like to share the responsibilities of running the household or bring up children. After Brati's death her plight became like a dead for about three months. Then to cope the situations she joined the service again. Though the family members resented. When she meets to Somu's mother who was Brati's comrade and Nandini, Brati's beloved, she comes to know that Brati and his comrades were betrayed by Anindya, their disguised companion. The massacre had left so many questions, unanswered! Was Brati's offence worse than all types of criminals that any one could kill him and his companions ? To kill them one did not need any social sanction from the law or the courts of justice! Was his offence so bad that he was shot dead so brutally! And even the faces of Brati and his companions were smashed so cruelly. Brati had decided for himself that freedom could not come from the path society and the state followed. He had lost faith in the social system itself. Brati had not remained content with writing slogans on the wall, he had come to commit himself to the slogans. There lay his offence. But why had had come to place such absolute faith in the cult of faithlessness. Is the burning faith in faithlessness that Brati and his compatriots had, destroyed by killing them ? Brati, who was for her the only legitimate excuse for going on living. She had become too possessive about Brati. It was Brati, who was alone under the care and love of his mother. Sujata had to strain a lot in the protection of her stubborn, sensitive and imaginative child from the dominance of her husband and her mother-in-law.

Now Brati is no more. There was ostentation, discipline and dummy social status. Sujata herself feels that she lived in a shiftless, rootless, lifeless and hypocritical society, where the naked body caused no embarrassment but natural emotions did. She could not cry aloud and lament before those whose first concern at her son's death was to hush up the news.

Brati's death was different from his companions and other's death. Different from Somu's, Laltu's, Partha's or Bijit's death! His name was not mentioned in the news or reports. The fate which was not destined for Brati, he made his own. He began to change not due to mere books or political lectures. He had felt the anguish of men like Somu and other poor who were humiliated by fate and life. He felt the anguish as keenly as if it was his own. Life itself had forced him to change. He gave up the life he was born to. He was reduced to mere numeral 1084. He was annihilated by own father. Though he could have found good job after the studies in Britain and make his well social status. It was inconsolable grief, a limitless void for Sujata. Her existence became barren.

Sujata was suffering of appendicitis. The doctor suspected her appendix to be gangrenous. If it was not removed at the proper time, it could develop gangrene. It could be worse if it burst. And at last the appendix was burst. It is the indication of her anguish and agony, which she suffered throughout her life. The pain before Brati's birth, the dominant and neglecting behaviour of her husband and mother-in-law, all her grief of her suppression, the same agony of her son's unfortunate death all that was gathered in her mind and heart as appendicitis. She could not help herself except living in her own world of imagination and talking to her dead son. This was more pain for her that her husband did not think important to identify the dead son, his mission was to hush up the news.

She could not know the other aspect of her son. It was of great pain for a mother who could not understand her son before his death. She could not check him from going outside though suspicion was there in her mind. She failed in controlling her son from his strayed path. Even after death she could not caress his face as it was battered and smashed by the blunt edge of a sharp, heavy weapon. The death took her closer to him. But the file on Brati Chatterjee was closed forever so abruptly. The news of Brati's death came on his birthday. Now Tuli's engagement is on the day of Brati's birthday. The day when he came to existence and the day also when he departed from the world. All this grief and anguish gathered in her heart. It was the culmination of her spiritual struggle when Saroj Pal, the Deputy Commissioner of Detective Department, Tuli's friend was invited to her own home. Saroj Pal who was on his duty and whose voice came through the telephone along with the news of Brati's death. Now Sujata herself had to offer the sweets to him. It was all surpassed by her capacity of bearing. Sujata's body fell to the ground. The appendix burst. The appendix of her body and of her mental anguish was burst.

REFERENCE

1. *Karl Marx.* 1946. *Selected Works.* Moscow: The Com. Publishers.

CONTRIBUTORS

A.D.N. Bajpai is a Professor of Economics at R.D. University, Jabalpur, M.P. Currently he is the Vice Chancellor of A.P.S. University, Rewa, Madhya Pradesh.

R.N. Rai is a Professor of English at B.H.U., Varanasi, Uttar Pradesh.

B.N. Singh is Professor and Head at the Dept. of English, Lucknow University, Uttar Pradesh.

Jagdev Singh is a Professor of English at the Punjab Agricultural University, Ludhiana, Punjab.

M.P. Sinha is Retd. Professor and Head of the Dept. of English, Kanpur University, Uttar Pradesh.

B.G. Tandon is Retd. Professor and Head of the Dept. of English, Vikram University, Ujjain, Madhya Pradesh.

Shubha Tiwari is Head of the Dept of English, A.P.S. University, Rewa, Madhya Pradesh.

Sadhana Agrawal is Asstt. Prof. of English at Maharaja College, Chhatarpur, Madhya Pradesh.

Ranjana Chanana is Asstt. Prof. of English at Maharaja College, Chhatarpur, Madhya Pradesh.

Anil Kumar Singh is Asstt. Prof. of English at S.G.S. College, Sidhi, Madhya Pradesh.

Vijay Prakash Singh is a Reader in the Dept. of English, Lucknow University, Lucknow, Uttar Pradesh.

Neelanjan Pathak is Asstt. Prof. of English at St. Aloysius College, Jabalpur, Madhya Pradesh.

Shobha Diwakar is Asstt. Prof. of English at C.P. Mahila Mahavidyalaya, Jabalpur, Madhya Pradesh.

Manjunatha Bevinakatti is a Reader in the Dept. of Folklore Studies, Kannada University, Hampi, Karnataka.

Aliya Shobi is a Research Scholar at the Dept. of English, G.G. University, Bilaspur, Madhya Pradesh.

Kiran Shukla is a Research Scholar at the Dept. of English, A.P.S. University, Rewa, Madhya Pradesh.

This anthology contains papers received for the U.G.C. National Seminar 2–3 February 2004 on 'Indian Fiction in English Translation' at the Department of English, A.P.S. University, Rewa-486 003, Madhya Pradesh, India.